KITCHENS AND BATHROOMS

Other Publications:

PLANET EARTH
COLLECTOR'S LIBRARY OF THE CIVIL WAR
LIBRARY OF HEALTH
CLASSICS OF THE OLD WEST
THE EPIC OF FLIGHT
THE GOOD COOK
THE SEAFARERS
THE ENCYCLOPEDIA OF COLLECTIBLES
THE GREAT CITIES
WORLD WAR II
THE WORLD'S WILD PLACES
THE TIME-LIFE LIBRARY OF BOATING
HUMAN BEHAVIOR
THE ART OF SEWING
THE OLD WEST
THE EMERGENCE OF MAN
THE AMERICAN WILDERNESS
THE TIME-LIFE ENCYCLOPEDIA OF GARDENING
LIFE LIBRARY OF PHOTOGRAPHY
THIS FABULOUS CENTURY
FOODS OF THE WORLD
TIME-LIFE LIBRARY OF AMERICA
TIME-LIFE LIBRARY OF ART
GREAT AGES OF MAN
LIFE SCIENCE LIBRARY
THE LIFE HISTORY OF THE UNITED STATES
TIME READING PROGRAM
LIFE NATURE LIBRARY
LIFE WORLD LIBRARY
FAMILY LIBRARY:
   HOW THINGS WORK IN YOUR HOME
   THE TIME-LIFE BOOK OF THE FAMILY CAR
   THE TIME-LIFE FAMILY LEGAL GUIDE
   THE TIME-LIFE BOOK OF FAMILY FINANCE

This volume is part of a series offering homeowners
detailed instructions on repairs, construction
and improvements they can undertake themselves.

HOME REPAIR
AND IMPROVEMENT

KITCHENS AND BATHROOMS

BY THE EDITORS OF
TIME-LIFE BOOKS

TIME-LIFE BOOKS
ALEXANDRIA, VIRGINIA

HOME REPAIR AND IMPROVEMENT

Editor	Philip W. Payne
Designer	Anne Masters

Editorial Staff for Kitchens and Bathrooms

Picture Editor	Adrian G. Allen
Text Editors	Mark M. Steele (principal), Lee Greene
Writers	Margaret Fogarty, Steven J. Forbis, Stuart Gannes, Kumait Jawdat, Brian McGinn, Mary Paul, Lydia Preston, Brooke C. Stoddard
Associate Designer	Abbe Stein
Art Associates	George Bell, Michelle Clay, Kenneth E. Hancock, Richard Whiting
Picture Coordinator	Rose-Mary Hall
Editorial Assistant	Eleanor G. Kask

Editorial Operations

Production Director	Feliciano Madrid
Assistants	Peter A. Inchauteguiz, Karen A. Meyerson
Copy Processing	Gordon E. Buck
Quality Control Director	Robert L. Young
Assistant	James J. Cox
Associates	Daniel J. McSweeney, Michael G. Wight
Art Coordinator	Anne B. Landry
Copy Room Director	Susan B. Galloway
Assistants	Celia Beattie, Ricki Tarlow

Correspondents: Elisabeth Kraemer (Bonn); Margot Hapgood, Dorothy Bacon (London); Susan Jonas, Lucy T. Voulgaris (New York); Maria Vincenza Aloisi, Josephine du Brusle (Paris); Ann Natanson (Rome). Valuable assistance was also provided by Carolyn T. Chubet, Miriam Hsia (New York).

THE CONSULTANTS: Robert F. Cox, the general consultant for this book, has owned a kitchen and bathroom remodeling business and worked in the field as a contractor for more than 25 years. He is chairman of the national Council of Certified Kitchen Designers and has written several manuals for bathroom and kitchen builders. He lectures widely at industry gatherings and teaches courses in bathroom contracting for professional designers.

Charles Crocker, plumbing consultant for the book, spent more than 25 years as a licensed plumber in Maryland, Virginia and the District of Columbia. A teacher of plumbing at Thomas A. Edison High School, Alexandria, Virginia, and chairman of the Arlington County Plumbing Board, he has run training programs for veterans and written several professional papers. He is now writing a plumbing textbook for high school and junior college students.

Harris Mitchell, special consultant for Canada, has worked in the field of home repair and improvement since 1950. He is Homes editor of *Today* magazine, writes a syndicated newspaper column, "You Wanted to Know," and is the author of a number of books on home improvement.

Gerard Drohan, a licensed master plumber, teaches basic plumbing at the Mechanics Institute in New York City.

Thomas D. Ball is a partner in a Maryland general contracting firm.

Richard Ridley, an architect, founded an architectural firm that has won awards for urban planning and residential building.

R. Daniel Nicholson Jr. is a construction manager specializing in home remodeling.

Roswell W. Ard, a civil engineer, is a consulting structural engineer and a professional home inspector.

Contents

A laminating tool to make neat edges. For fast and neat trimming of plastic laminate on countertops and vanity tops, a router is convenient though not essential. Edge strips are applied first, then trimmed flush to the top, bottom and edges of the counter core; the ¹⁄₁₆-inch surface sheet is cemented in place and trimmed flush to the edge strips.

No rooms are more used—and abused—than kitchens and bathrooms. Their floors carry the heaviest traffic; their cabinets are attacked by heat, moisture, acids and alkalies; their walls are splashed by cleaning agents and grease, and drenched by water and steam. The rigors of this environment must be taken into account in all aspects of renovating these rooms, or building new ones, for such conditions affect every step of the work from planning to carpentry, plumbing and electrical installations (*Chapters 2, 3 and 4*). But the major consideration is the surface—floors, walls and countertops. In kitchens and bathrooms their coverings are special. They have to be.

A surprisingly large selection of materials is now available to protect and beautify the exposed surfaces of these difficult rooms. New materials, such as synthetic marble, come in kits (*pages 36-39*), and improved adhesives enable an amateur to practice the ancient art of tile setting (*pages 22-27*) or the modern one of plastic lamination (*pages 30-35*). A choice among the materials depends partly on economics and partly on esthetics, but also on practical considerations of durability, application methods, comfort and safety.

The most comfortable and least expensive kitchen floor coverings are resilient materials such as rolled sheet vinyl (*pages 14-19*). Bathroom floors, however, are so often wet that ceramic tile, which is impervious to moisture, is commonly used there; a marble threshold (*page 21*) is advisable to stop water from seeping under a door.

The main surface of a work space offers the widest choice of all. An ideal countertop material would be stainproof, impervious to moisture, scratch resistant, unaffected by heat, slightly resilient, good to look at and reasonably priced. Every popular material combines some, but not all, of these characteristics. Ceramic tile is hard, moistureproof and heat resistant—but the crevices between tiles collect dirt and carelessly handled dishes or bottles may break on the hard surface. Plastic laminates are resilient, nonporous and resistant to grease and household chemicals—but they are easily damaged by knife scratches or hot pans. Synthetic marble is handsome and virtually stainproof, but it is expensive, and less heat resistant than tile.

All these materials have also been used on walls, but there their toughness is crucial only in areas that may be splashed. Elsewhere another factor is worth weighing: noise. Impervious materials bounce sounds to increase the din in rooms that are already very noisy. Wallpaper or paint, while hardly sound absorbent, add less to noise than special materials. In any case, esthetics generally dictate wall coverings; in many stylish kitchens and bathrooms in the 1970s, walls were paneled in wood—a material noted neither for sound absorbency nor resistance to a moist, chemically laden environment.

Smoothing the Way for New Walls and Floors

Renovating a kitchen or a bathroom wall or floor begins with creating a clean, sound, level subsurface. This usually involves removing or repairing the existing finished surface—plaster, wallboard, tile, linoleum or wood—and then applying the new finish.

Depending on the extent of your renovations, preparing a wall may require building additional framing *(pages 96-100)* or installing special waterproof wallboard around a tub or shower *(page 103)*. Except for these special cases, however, you will probably need only to patch a few holes or cracks in your wall, reseat any popped nails, reattach any loose wallboard and possibly remove wallpaper before applying a new finish. Fill any holes and small cracks with vinyl spackling compound or wallboard joint cement. To repair larger damaged areas of wallboard, cut out the damaged section from stud to stud and nail in a new piece.

Patch plaster walls similarly. Fill shallow depressions with several layers of spackling compound or joint cement and sand smooth. Smash big bulges with a hammer and patch the resulting hole. If the plaster is rough, stippled or undulating, you can nail furring strips to the studs through the plaster and attach wallboard to achieve a smooth surface. But if the room cannot accommodate the extra thickness, or if the plaster has deteriorated beyond repair, remove the plaster and the lath and attach wallboard.

Floors take more punishment than walls and often require more extensive preparation. A kitchen or a bathroom floor, like most house floors, is usually a three-layered sandwich. A subfloor is laid over and attached directly to the joists. It may consist of tongue-and-groove lumber laid diagonally across the joists, or sheets of exterior-grade plywood, usually ⅝ inch thick. The underlayment, laid over and attached to the subfloor, may be of hardboard or particle board of various thicknesses, although ⅜-inch exterior-grade plywood is frequently used in the kitchen or bathroom for its superior water-resistant qualities. On top of the underlayment is the finish flooring.

If the finish flooring is in reasonably good shape you may be able to lay the new directly over the old. Badly deteriorated finish flooring must be removed or covered with new underlayment. Though the latter remedy adds height as well as cost to the new floor, and may require trimming of door bottoms, it is generally quicker and easier than removing stubborn tiles or linoleum.

Make sure the existing finish flooring does not conceal decay below. Search for loose or broken tiles, lifting and curling seams, buckling, dampness, odors, discoloration or other signs of moisture under sinks and lavatories and around tubs, dishwashers and toilets.

Water seeps readily through minuscule pinholes and cracks along seams and edges. The wax ring that seals a toilet bowl to its mounting flange is a common site of leaks; to check thoroughly around a toilet you must remove the bowl *(page 92, Step 1)*.

Anywhere the floor feels suspiciously soft or yielding, remove a section of finish flooring and probe for rot with a screwdriver. Depending on the extent of the damage, you may need to patch *(pages 10-11)* or replace *(pages 12-13)* the underlayment, the subfloor or both.

Removing floor molding. Before you add or subtract a layer of flooring, remove the base shoe, the rounded strip attached to the floor. Beginning near the center of the wall, pry it out enough with a thin blade to admit the end of a utility bar. Working along the wall in both directions, dislodge the base shoe a half inch or so, dropping in small wood wedges as you go, until the base shoe is free. Similarly remove the baseboard.

If you intend to reuse brittle molding, work carefully. If molding starts to split, drive the nail that is splitting it on through with a nail set. Loosen vinyl cove molding at one end with a putty knife and peel it away from the wall; it probably cannot be salvaged.

Preparing the surface. Before laying underlayment or finish flooring over an existing floor, clean the floor thoroughly. All dirt and old wax must be removed; a floor sander will speed the job. Rebond loose vinyl tiles by applying a hot iron, protecting the tile surface with an old towel (*below*). If heat fails to reactivate the adhesive, lift the tile, scrape up the old adhesive and reset the tile with new adhesive. Fill the spaces left by missing or broken tiles with plaster of paris.

Removing ceramic tile. Wear safety goggles when removing ceramic tile from a wall or a floor. Begin where you can work the edge of a cold chisel under the edge of a tile. To make a start, you may have to smash one tile with a hammer and chisel out the fragments. Then work on the edges of adjoining tiles with gentle taps on the chisel. By working gently you minimize damage to the subsurface and avoid much patching and filling later.

When repairing a tiled surface before laying a new surface over it, fill the spaces left by broken or missing tiles with plaster of paris. Reattach loose tiles with adhesive (*page 27*).

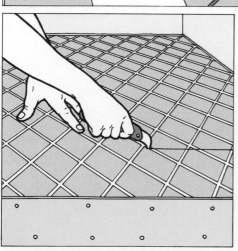

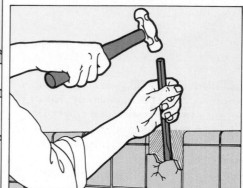

Removing old flooring. To remove continuous flooring such as linoleum or cushioned vinyl, cut it into strips of manageable size with a utility or linoleum knife and then peel or roll it up. Some will come easily, some will have to be coaxed with a stiff-bladed scraper. (Scrapers sold as lawn edgers or ice chippers work well, and may serve even better if sharpened.)

Heat vinyl tiles with an iron to liquefy the adhesive, then pry them up. Cold will also break the bond; some professionals put a block of dry ice on a tile for a few seconds, then pry it up. If you use this method, keep the room well ventilated and avoid touching the ice with bare hands. After removing the finish flooring, scrape any remaining adhesive off the underlayment.

Installing new underlayment. Plywood and the hardboard commonly used for underlayment come in 4-by-4 and 4-by-8-foot sheets. Arrange the underlayment in a staggered pattern (*above*) of whole sheets and fractions of sheets that avoids the alignment of joints and that spans all the joints in the subfloor. To allow for expansion, separate the sheets from one another by about 1/32 inch and leave about 1/8 inch between the outside edges of the underlayment and the walls. Fasten each sheet with fourpenny resin-coated nails; they should be spaced 4 inches apart over the whole surface of the sheet and set in 3/8 inch from the edges.

Patching the Subfloor and Underlayment

You can repair minor damage in underlayment and subfloor by replacing damaged portions with patches. Remove all the old finish flooring. Plan your patches so that the joints of an underlayment patch do not coincide with the joints of the subflooring. Thus, when patching the subfloor, be sure to cut out an area of underlayment larger than the patch you intend to make in the subfloor. When patching only the underlayment, cut out enough old underlayment so that the patch will span all subfloor beneath it.

Most patching is straightforward and, with a few carpentry tricks, you can easily patch around through-the-floor obstacles like the toilet flange opposite.

Before sawing up portions of the floor, turn off the power to all circuits running to or through the room to avert the danger of accidentally severing a live wire.

Patching plywood subfloor. Remove the finish flooring around the damaged area and saw out a segment of underlayment larger than your proposed patch. Cut out a segment of subfloor, cutting back to the center of the nearest joist on the sides of the damaged area that run parallel to the joists. Patch the hole with plywood subflooring nailed to the joists, and over that a piece of underlayment nailed to the subflooring. Make sure the patches match the thicknesses of the existing subfloor and underlayment.

Patching tongue-and-groove subflooring. Remove finish flooring and then saw out a segment of underlayment around the damaged area, and larger than the proposed patch. Cut each damaged subfloor board at the center of the nearest joist. Saw the tongue off one of the damaged boards and pry the board out. Then pry out the remaining boards, leaving a diamond-shaped hole and exposing the tongue edge of a board at one side. Trim off the tongue. Attach a plywood patch, the size and shape of the hole, to the joists. Patch the hole in the underlayment as shown above, making sure the finished work is flush with the rest of the floor.

Note: Subfloor boards are usually ⅝ inch thick and can be replaced with ⅝-inch plywood. In an old house the boards may be of an odd thickness and you may have to shim beneath the plywood patch to make it flush.

Patching underlayment. After removing the finish flooring, poke a chisel or a screwdriver through a soft spot in the underlayment to determine its thickness and set your circular saw to that depth. Saw out and remove a square or rectangle of underlayment around the damaged area. Attach a patch of the same size, shape and thickness to the subfloor.

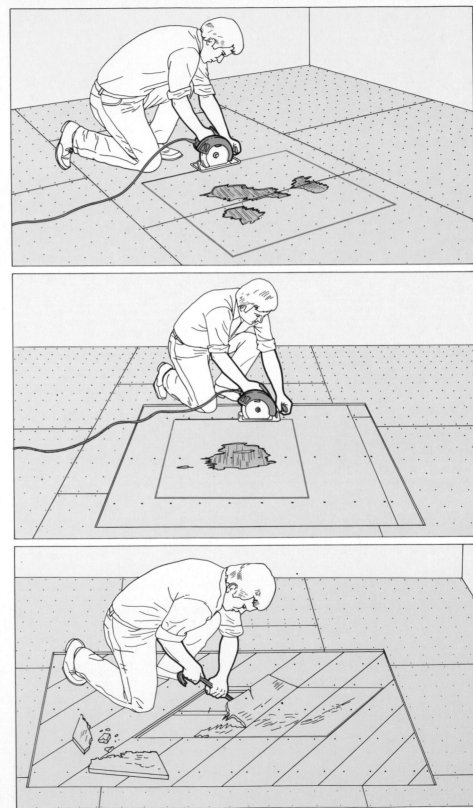

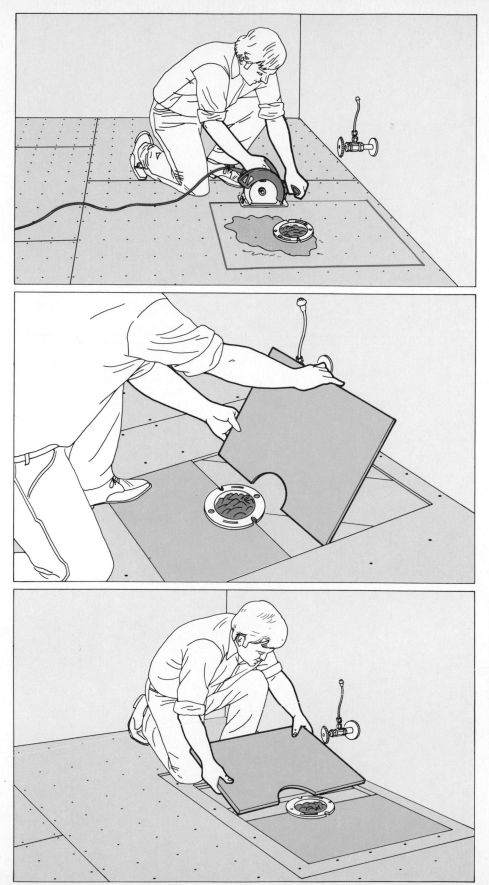

The Trouble Spots around a Toilet

Removing damaged underlayment. Remove the toilet *(page 92, Step 1)* and stuff the flange with rags to eliminate odors and possible loss of small tools. Remove the finish flooring and saw out a section of underlayment around the damaged area. Remove any screws attaching the toilet-mounting flange to the floor. Remove the cutout underlayment, easing it out from under the flange without putting upward pressure on the flange. Avoid disturbing the joint between the flange and the drain beneath; the joint is watertight but not structurally sound.

Replacing underlayment. Cut a patch the size and shape of the hole you have made in the underlayment. Cut a hole in the patch of the right size, shape and position to fit around the flange when the patch is installed. You can determine the position of the hole in the patch by measuring to the flange from each side of the hole cut for the patch in the underlayment. Cut the patch in two along a line that bisects the hole in the patch, making sure that this line does not coincide with a joint in the subfloor. Slip the two pieces of patch into place under the flange and nail them to the subfloor.

Repairing subfloor. Remove finish flooring and underlayment from around the damaged area. Cut out subflooring along the centers of the nearest joists and back to the wall behind the toilet. Remove the damaged material as in removing damaged underlayment *(top)*. Cut a patch the size and shape of the hole in the subfloor—square or rectangular if you have a plywood subfloor, diamond shaped in the case of tongue and groove as shown at left. Cut a hole for the flange, divide the patch through the center of the hole and fit it around the flange *(center)*. Nail the patch to the joists. Patch the underlayment.

Replacing a Damaged Floor

If your floor is so damaged that you must replace it completely, begin by removing floor molding and finish flooring. If the tub rests directly on the joists, leave it in place; old flooring can be pulled from around it. If the tub rests on the subfloor, check the condition of the floor underneath; if it is still good, leave this portion intact and remove old flooring around it. In all other cases disconnect and remove the tub (pages 92-93).

Determine the combined thickness of underlayment and subfloor, and set your circular saw to this depth. Turn off power to circuits entering or passing through the room. Cut through the flooring all around the room, as close to the walls as possible. Most saws will get within 1½ inches. Beginning at a side of the room opposite a door, pry up and remove the underlayment and subflooring. Remove all nails from the joists. When all the joists are exposed, throw down two or three sheets of subfloor material as a temporary work surface and inspect every joist. If there are any signs of rot, small areas an inch or so deep can be cut away and the surrounding wood treated with preservative. Signs of extensive rot call for a professional survey.

1 **Installing cleats.** Removing the old flooring will expose all of the floor joists except the outer two, which will remain hidden under the walls at two opposite sides of the room. To provide a bearing surface for the new floor on those sides, attach two 2-by-4s to each hidden joist. Nail one 2-by-4 to the joist, then nail the second one to the first. Drill a ⅜-inch hole through both 2-by-4s and into the joist. You must secure these cleats with ⅜-inch lag screws 6 inches long topped with 1-inch washers.

A warped tilting joist can often be brought back to vertical by yoking it to an adjoining joist with a 2-by-6 header (inset).

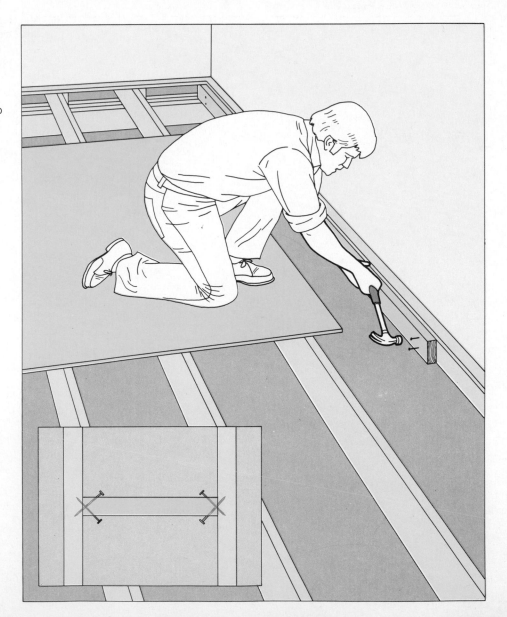

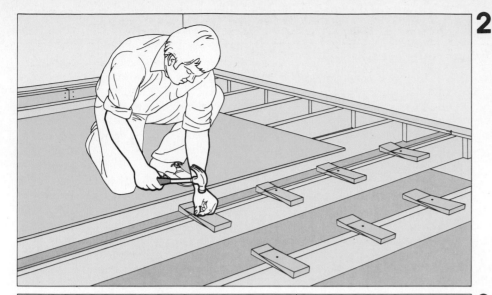

2 **Preparing for the subfloor.** If one joist seems lower than the rest, check along its length and at both ends for damage. If it has simply warped or sagged, restore it to proper level with "horsefeathers," paired wedge-shaped shims. Using a string as a straightedge, move the shims together until the desired height is reached and secure them with a nail. Place shims every foot or so as far as the sag extends. If the joist seems warped throughout most of its length, spike a "sister" joist to its side at the proper level.

3 **Planning subfloor installation.** Before installing the subfloor, plan to lay the plywood sheets so that you use as many full sheets as possible while avoiding alignment of joints. Trim sheets as necessary so that when the edges of two sheets meet at a joist there is nailing surface for both. Lay each panel in place; at each joist it covers draw a line down its length as a nailing guide. Remove the panel and apply a ribbon of construction adhesive on each joist (following the manufacturer's instructions).

4 **Laying subfloor and underlayment.** Nail the subflooring to the joists with coated No. 8 box nails. Space the nails 6 inches apart at the ends of sheets and ⅜ inches from the edges. Space nails 10 inches apart between the edges of each sheet. Where the ends of two panels meet at a joist, stagger the nails to keep from splitting the joist. Begin applying underlayment at the end of the room opposite to the end at which you started laying subflooring. Arrange the underlayment so that the panels overlap the seams of the subflooring. Attach the underlayment as shown on page 9. Fit subflooring and underlayment around the toilet flange of a toilet as described on page 11.

Rolled Flooring: Seamless and Easy on the Feet

Years ago, rolled sheets of flooring were made of only one material—linoleum. Today the material is almost certain to be sheet vinyl—easy to maintain and install.

Sheet vinyl comes in two basic types: inlaid, in which the pattern is pressed through the vinyl; and rotogravure, or "roto" for short, in which the pattern is printed on the surface. Both come in compositions of differing resiliency, some so flexible you can roll them into a ball and others so brittle they split if you try to press them into a corner.

Of the two types roto offers the greater variety of colors and patterns. It is softer and more nearly soundproof, because its wear surface is thin and the vinyl sheet has a thick foam-rubber backing called fatback. It is available in 6-, 12- and occasionally 9- and 15-foot widths—an advantage, because the variety of widths

virtually eliminates the need for seaming, the most difficult part of laying sheet vinyl. But roto's softness makes it easier to puncture, and some furniture—a kitchen table, for instance—can leave a permanent indentation if left too long in one spot. Inlaid sheet vinyl is harder and more durable, but it usually comes only in 6-foot rolls.

As the first step in an installation make a plan of the floor, marking the dimensions. Add 6 inches at each wall for overlap and note the width of the pattern repetition, usually printed on the back of the sheet, if you must seam sheets together. The allowance for seaming equals this width; for example, if your pattern repeats every 3 feet, allow 3 feet of extra width when you buy the material.

Remove the shoe molding (page 8) from the baseboard and generally the

baseboard, too; it is best replaced with cove molding (page 20). Remove all the old wax and sweep the floor clean.

When returning heavy appliances, such as the refrigerator, to the room after the vinyl has been laid, push them back on top of a sheet of hardboard to avoid making deep, permanent ridges in the vinyl.

Leave the fitting of the vinyl to a threshold for the final step of the job. At an existing marble or wood threshold, cut the vinyl as close to the threshold as possible, shaving a little at a time to arrive at a close fit. If there is no threshold, or if you are planning to replace it, use metal edging strips, which is the best transition from new vinyl flooring to the floor covering in an adjoining room. If you use a metal tuck-in strip as a threshold (page 21), leave the vinyl edge in the doorway unglued until the strip is installed.

1 **Rolling out the material.** Let the material adjust to room temperature for an hour or so; then, if you are using more than one sheet of material, start unrolling the larger sheet from the longest and most nearly clear wall of the room. Leave 3 to 6 inches of overlap at each wall.

When you reach a large immovable object, such as a center island or a set of built-in cabinets, reach under the roll and unroll the sheet backward toward the starting wall. Push the unrolled section of the sheet against the object and, about 6 inches above the floor, cut the sheet from its outside edge toward its center with a utility knife. Continue the cut about 6 inches short of the edge of the object, then cut back toward the starting wall for a distance at least 6 inches less than the object's depth.

2 **Fitting around a large object.** Lift the roll over the object and lower it to the floor on the other side. Holding the corner of the flap you have made in the sheet, complete the cutout for the object by cutting, if necessary, to a point about 6 inches from its far edge, then cutting at a right angle toward the outside edge of the sheet.

3 **Fitting around a small object.** Roll the material past a pipe *(near right)* or other small obstruction and slice a slit from the nearest edge of the material to the object. Carefully carve a circle around the object, making several cuts if necessary, then press the sheet together behind the object. If the slit is long, seal the seam *(Step 15)*. For a neat job, slide the base ring up the pipe before laying the vinyl, then return it to the finished floor; if the pipe does not have a base ring, use the model shown here, which snaps around the pipe and screws to the floor.

To cut around a toilet flange in a bathroom, feel for the edges of the flange beneath the material and cut around the flange until all of it is exposed *(far right)*. The cut need not be exact: the toilet bowl will overlap the flange, covering any ragged edges.

4 **Reversing the roll.** Unroll the sheet completely, pull it back upon itself and reroll the sheet back from the far edge with the underside of the sheet inside the roll. (The tight original roll in this area compresses the pattern; unless the roll is reversed briefly, the pattern will be smaller in one part of the room than the other.) Unroll the sheet again and press the material into all corners, to the extent that its natural resiliency will allow. Caution: Do not try to force brittle material into a corner; it will split if pressed too tightly.

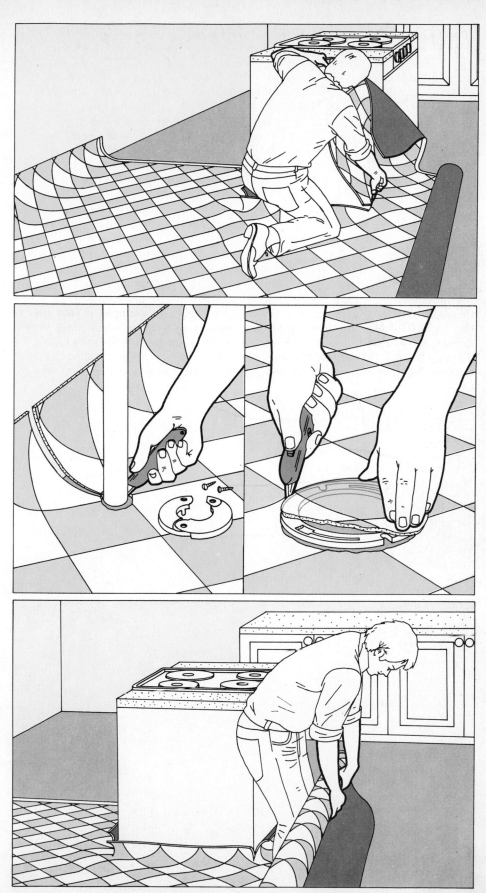

5 **Laying the second sheet.** Measure the width of uncovered floor from the edge of the first sheet to the wall; to this distance add 6 inches plus the amount of overlap required to match the pattern. Mark the total distance on the second sheet and cut off any excess material.

Roll the second sheet out halfway, then pull it over the first sheet until the patterns match. Unroll the rest of the second sheet as you did the first, cutting around objects.

6 **Trimming the edges.** Pull the second sheet off the first and out of the way. At each wall and object, cut the material back to about 3 inches above the floor. Caution: take care in making this cut—you are now close to the final trim.

7 **Applying the adhesive.** Pull the first sheet halfway back upon itself. Using a trowel with 1/16-inch grooves, spread adhesive over the floor; do not cover a 6-inch strip along the line at which the first sheet will meet the second, but work the adhesive into corners as closely as possible. Follow the manufacturer's recommendations for the choice of an adhesive and any instructions on its use; his guarantee may depend upon strict adherence to his advice.

At the completion of this step, go on to the next immediately: after about 45 minutes most adhesives become so sticky that the material is hard to adjust.

8 Setting the vinyl in place. Lift the edge of the rolled material high above the floor and slowly walk it back into place over the adhesive. Lay it against the wall and press it into place at the corners as closely as its resiliency will allow.

9 Rolling out the bumps. Using an ordinary rolling pin and starting from the center, roll the material toward each of its edges. Work slowly, and be sure to flatten any bulges or air bubbles that have risen above the flat surface.

10 Making the final cuts. Press a metal yardstick hard along the lines where walls or objects meet the floor, creasing the material sharply at the corners, then slice the material at the wall along the edge of the yardstick with a utility knife. You may not be able to crease inlaid sheet vinyl sharply at a first try; instead, make repeated cuts until the vinyl fits the corner. Caution: Normally, molding will cover cutting errors to about ½ inch from the wall, but ceramic cove molding is not removed before laying the vinyl; for this type of molding the cuts must be exact.

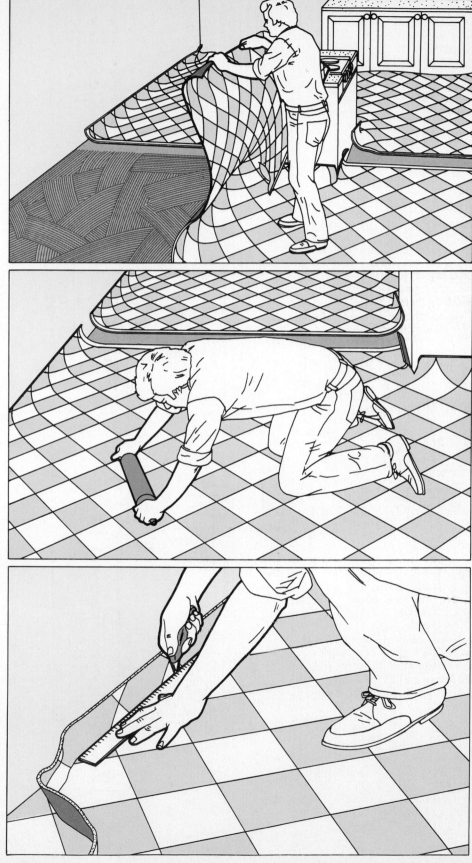

11 Cutting off the trim. Place a metal yardstick along the overlapping edge of the second vinyl sheet and cut off the ½- to 1-inch trim at the edge of the sheet. On inlaid vinyl this trim is likely to be an extra-wide grout line: Cut along the line to bring its width down to that of the other grout lines in the pattern.

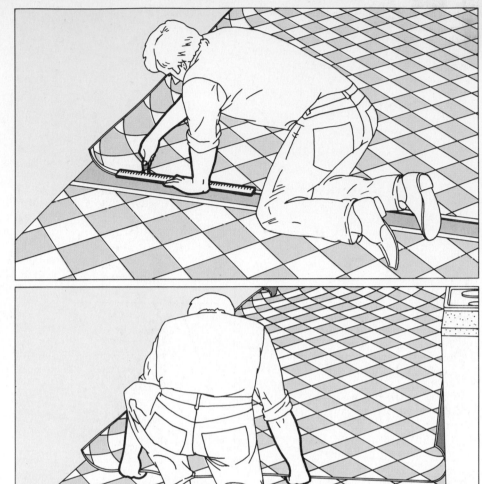

12 Matching the pattern. Pull the second sheet over the first until the patterns of the two sheets match perfectly. Caution: Note the pattern carefully to be sure the overlap continues the pattern in the same manner—a mismatched pattern will spoil the appearance of the finished job.

13 Cutting off the overlap. Place a metal yardstick along the edge of the top sheet and, holding a utility knife straight up and down and using the yardstick as a guide, cut through the bottom sheet. Pull the top sheet back and remove the strip you have cut from the bottom.

If the material you are using is resilient enough to permit a cut through two sheets at once, overlap the second sheet to a segment of pattern repetition and, using a yardstick as a guide, cut through both sheets at once. This method assures a perfect match of the pattern.

Lay the second sheet as you did the first, cutting overlaps of 3 to 6 inches around objects, spreading the adhesive to within 6 inches of the edge of the first sheet and making a final trim along each wall and object.

14 **Applying adhesive under the seam.** Check the manufacturer's directions for sealing the seam between two sheets (*Step 15, below*). If he does not call for seam sealer below the sheets, simply pull back the butted edges on both sheets and spread adhesive over the bare floor along the entire length of the seam. Then, while the adhesive is still plastic, push the sheets back into place, pressing the edges together until you get a tight fit. Go on immediately to the next step.

15 **Sealing the seam.** Press the seam together with the thumb and fingers of one hand while applying seam sealer with the other. Most seam sealers are applied with a T-shaped nozzle (*inset*) with the top of the T riding on top of the material and the bottom inside the seam. Caution: Some manufacturers require that sealing be applied beneath the seam—consult the manufacturer's directions for sealing before carrying out Step 14, above. For either method, wipe away all excess sealing immediately and do not step on the seam for 24 hours.

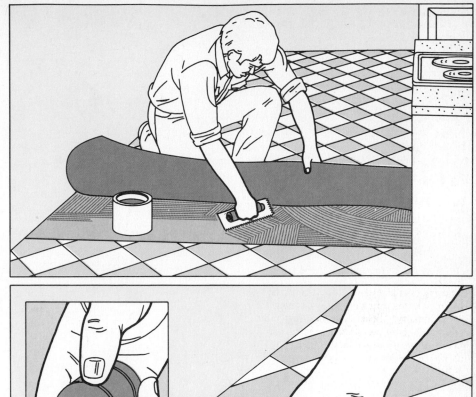

Softer Yet—Carpeting

Although the trend is toward sheet vinyl or tile flooring in bathrooms and kitchens, some people prefer carpeting, particularly in bathrooms—and with good reasons. Carpeting is soft underfoot, and creates a feeling of luxury and warm comfort. But it has its disadvantages. It is not as durable as good tile or vinyl, is easily stained and can be ruined by an overflow of water.

If you choose carpeting for the kitchen or the bathroom, remember the ever-present moisture in those rooms. Select a carpeting that has the tightest possible weave—the heavier the carpeting gauge, as indicated on the back of the sample, the tighter the weave and the more impervious the material will be to spills.

Carpeting is usually fastened to the floor with double-faced tape rather than adhesive. After clearing the floor, lay the tape along the edges of the room and all permanently installed objects. Cut the carpeting to fit the room as you would sheet vinyl, pull half the carpeting back upon itself and peel the top paper from the tape. Walk the carpet back into place, and press it down; repeat the process for the other half.

A Molding Curved for Cleaning

Vinyl cove base, molded as a single concave strip so that it is easy to clean and moisture resistant, is more practical than wood baseboard for edging rolled flooring. It comes in 2-, 4- and 6-inch widths in straight sections 48 inches long; also available are premolded corners. It is sold in a variety of colors and can be cleaned and waxed as part of the flooring. Use a 6-inch strip for the best protection against mopping and splashes; a 4-inch strip will just fill the kick space beneath a standard kitchen cabinet.

Installation is simple, but you must take special precautions with the special adhesive, which is noxious and highly flammable. Turn off all the electrical appliances (including the refrigerator and the freezer) and the pilot lights of a gas range before beginning the job; do not smoke; be sure that all of the windows and doors are wide open; and keep the can of adhesive covered as much as possible, transferring small quantities of the adhesive, as needed, from the can to a piece of scrap plywood.

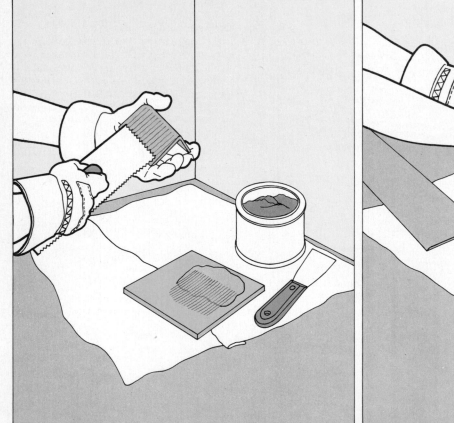

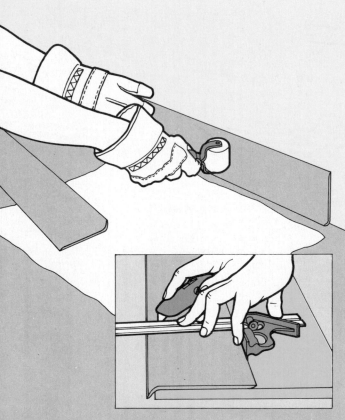

Installing a corner piece. Cover the floor with dropcloths or newspapers, then begin the installation at an inside corner. Using a 3-inch trowel with notches 1/16 inch deep, apply vinyl adhesive evenly to the wide vertical surface of an inside corner piece; the short curved edge that rests on the floor need not be glued. Caution: This adhesive is hazardous; follow the safety instructions in the text above. Fit the piece carefully into the corner. The adhesive will hold it almost immediately and will harden in about 10 minutes. Remove excess adhesive from the wall with a rag soaked in soap and water.

Installing the straight sections. Apply adhesive to the vertical side of a straight 4-foot section of cove base and lay the section along the longest wall adjoining the corner piece. Butt it carefully, then press it against the wall with a steel handroller (above) available from your flooring supplier. Add straight sections until you are within 4 feet of the end of the wall. Install the next corner piece and measure a straight length to fill the gap, plus 1/16 inch to ensure a tight fit. To cut this length, true a combination square against the top edge of the cove and make repeated cuts along it with a utility knife (inset).

Thresholds to Mate Materials

The last step in installing a kitchen or bathroom floor is to cover the seams in doorways where the edge of the new flooring material meets adjoining surfaces. In bathrooms, where water spillage is commonplace, raised thresholds act as miniature dams to keep water from seeping under the door and damaging adjacent wood floors or carpeting. Although wood, metal and even rubber thresholds are available, the favored material is traditional marble. Marble is difficult to trim and must be bought in the exact length needed to fit between the bathroom doorjambs *(below)*.

In kitchens, three types of metal edging are used to edge vinyl flooring. The binder bar—usually a slightly curved aluminum strip 1½ inches wide—simply covers a seam. A narrower L-shaped edging protects the vinyl edge where it abuts abrasive surfaces like brick or concrete. The tuck-in, or gripper bar *(inset, bottom)*, used where vinyl meets carpeting, provides a narrow slot into which the carpeting can be tucked and secured.

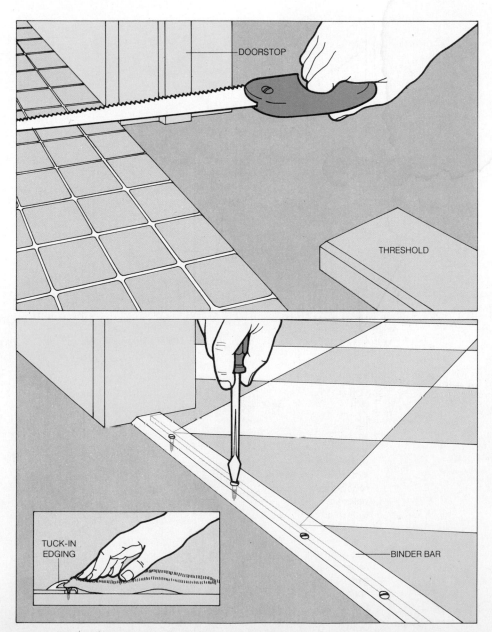

Setting marble thresholds. Place the threshold, sized to fit between the doorjambs, on the old floor surface and mark its height on the doorstops. Using a keyhole saw, cut the doorstops at the marks. Use a wood chisel, if necessary, to remove the pieces. Spread ceramic-tile adhesive between the doorjambs and along the bottom of the threshold. Then fit the threshold under the trimmed doorstops until it is butted against the floor tiles *(pages 24-25)*. Clean off the excess adhesive and let the threshold set at least three hours before grouting.

Installing metal edging. When using binder bar, cut it to fit the opening. Place it directly over the seam between the two flooring materials and screw it to the subfloor. Do not screw into tiles, which may crack; trim the tiles if necessary, so that the screws go directly into the floor.

L-shaped edging is laid over the vinyl edge and screwed through it into the subfloor. Tuck-in edging *(inset)* is screwed to subflooring so that carpeting can be tucked snugly into the slotted side while the other side covers the edge of the vinyl floor covering.

Ceramic Tile: Impervious and Permanent

Ceramic tiles of tough fired clay make a durable, beautiful, impervious surface for walls, floors or countertops. Smooth and shiny glazed tiles are commonly used on walls and countertops; unglazed tiles, less slippery and less easily marred by wear, are better for floors.

Tiles are usually square or hexagonal, range in size from 1 to 12 inches square and come in a wide selection of colors. In addition, a variety of trim tile is available. Most tiles have projections on their edges to space them from their neighbors. Some are designed to fill interior corners where two tile surfaces meet; they are often used instead of baseboard on tiled walls. Other types of trim tiles have rounded edges to give the last row of a surface a finished look or to go around corners and the counter edges.

Laying ceramic tiles involves preparing a smooth surface (pages 8-13), planning a pattern and attaching the tiles with adhesive. (The ancient technique of setting tiles in mortar—"mud" in the tilesetter's jargon—is still widely used by professionals for both indoor and outdoor work and by amateurs on outdoor jobs like tiling a patio; using mud indoors is tricky work best left to experts.)

Tile adhesives include cement-based mortars, epoxies, latex-mortar and epoxy-mortar combinations and organic adhesives. Most popular with amateur tilesetters are the organics, which are relatively inexpensive, work well for residential tiling, require no mixing and are easier to apply than epoxies.

When buying adhesive, consult a dealer and read the label on the container to make sure the product fits your needs as to bonding ability, setting time and water resistance. Most tile adhesives will bond tile to most other surfaces, but there are exceptions; to lay ceramic tile directly over vinyl floor tile, for instance, you need an epoxy adhesive.

Floor adhesives usually harden more quickly than wall adhesives. Thus you can spread adhesive over a large area of wall before setting tile; you must spread floor adhesive a little at a time, but you can walk on a floor 24 hours after tiling it.

Wall adhesives are either Type I, which resists prolonged wetting and should be used around tubs and showers, or Type II, which stands up to intermittent wetting and can be used behind a backsplash. Before tiling any surface that will be wetted frequently, seal it with a thin coat of adhesive (page 24).

After being set in adhesive, the tiles are leveled and the spaces between them are filled with grout—a decorative mortar available in many colors—that seals out dirt and water. Consult a dealer and read the label to make sure you get a suitable grout. Some tiles, for instance, require a silicone grout (page 27).

Mix mortar-type grout to the consistency recommended by the manufacturer. Mortar-type grouts must dry slowly to "cure," or harden properly. Some floor tiles steal water from grout and impede curing. Before grouting, put a drop of water on the back of a tile; if the tile soaks it up, use more water in the grout.

To make floor grout joints flush with tile surfaces fill the joints with a grout containing a water-retaining aggregate, sprinkle dry grout of the same kind over the grout joints and rub the joints with a piece of burlap, using a circular motion.

After tiling a floor, cover it with poly-ethylene sheeting. If no condensation appears under the sheeting the next day, remove it, sprinkle water on the floor and replace the sheeting. Let the grout cure for three days. After 10 days seal the grout joints with a sealer sold to protect the grout from dirt or mildew.

For easier installation, small tiles called mosaic tiles are sold attached to sheets of paper or mesh 1-by-1 or 1-by-2 feet in size. Larger wall tiles also can be bought in sheets already grouted (page 26). A dealer will tell you how much tile you need if you bring him a sketch showing the shape and dimensions of the area to be covered. Be sure to get enough—and a little extra. Colors and patterns come on and go off the market fairly frequently and even the same color may vary from batch to batch.

Only simple tools are required—a level and chalk line for laying out tilework, a square for keeping it straight and a notched trowel for spreading adhesive. Buy a trowel with notches the size and spacing specified on the label of the adhesive container. For cutting the large unglazed tiles called quarry tiles, rent a heavy-duty tile cutter such as professionals use. For glazed tiles you can use a glass cutter for scoring straight cuts, and for cutting curves and angles get a pair of nippers, a cutting tool similar to pliers that nibbles away tiles a bit at a time. A carbide-tipped hole saw can save you time and work in making large numbers of round holes, as for fitting tile around pipe. Protect your eyes with safety glasses when using nippers or a hole saw.

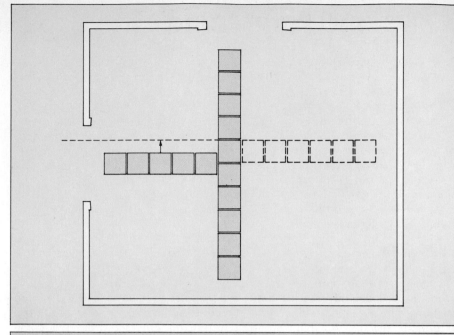

Fitting the Pattern to the Room

Planning a pattern for a floor. Lay a row of dry tile—or squares of tiles—from the middle of a doorway to the opposite wall, guided by a string nailed from the doorway to the wall. If a gap of less than half a tile width remains at the end of the run, remove the first tile and center the remaining tiles. The resulting spaces left for the two border tiles will equal more than half the width of a tile, avoiding awkward cuts on tiny pieces.

If the room has a second doorway, run a second row of tiles inward from this doorway until it nearly reaches the first row of tiles. Slide the first row over until its edge meets the last tile of the second row. Snap intersecting chalk lines as a guide for laying the tiles.

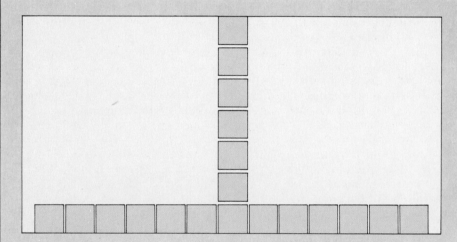

Planning a countertop pattern. Lay a row of dry tiles across the front edge of the counter. Lay a second row perpendicular to the first from the front edge to the backsplash. Adjust the positions of the two rows as at left above so that border tiles are even. If only a small amount of space remains at either of the borders, arrange the tiles slightly farther apart and plan to fill the spaces between them with grout after the tiles have been cemented in place.

Positioning tiles on a wall. Since horizontal features—tub rim, floor edges, floor cove moldings or countertop—are almost never truly level, use a level to find the lowest point at which the feature meets the wall. Measure one tile width above this point, plus ¼ inch for clearance under the tiles, and snap a chalk line the length of the wall. Find the highest point of the horizontal feature and measure its distance from the chalk line. If this distance is within ⅛ inch of a tile height, align the tops of the first row of tiles with the chalk line and vary the size of its joint line beneath the tiles. If the distance from the high point to the chalk line is not within ⅛ inch of the tile height, trim tiles to fit between the line and the horizontal feature.

Determine the width of border tiles by measuring the length of the wall and calculating how many whole tiles will fill that space while leaving room for borders more than half a tile wide.

The Tricks of Cutting

Cutting border tiles. Lay a dry tile over the last fixed tile next to the border. Place another dry tile on top of it and move the second tile to the wall, leaving a grout-line space equal to that between other tiles. Mark the first tile where the top tile overlaps it. This portion should fit the border space. Cut at the mark with a tile cutter or score the tile with a glass cutter, using a straightedge as a guide. Place the tile over a pencil, lining up the pencil with the scored line on the tile. Press gently on both sides of the tile until it breaks. If the tile is scored too close to the edge to break easily, use tile nippers.

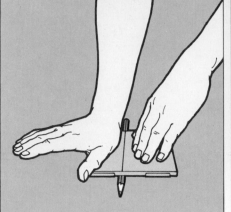

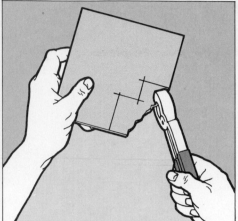

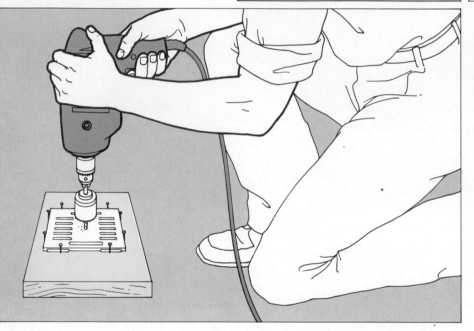

Making irregular cuts. When cutting tile to fit around a doorjamb or other irregular area, first mark the line of the cut. Holding the tile glazed side up, use nippers to nibble away the unwanted part of the tile. Practice using nippers on waste tile before making an unfamiliar cut. Take tiny bites—less than ⅛ inch at a time—to avoid breaking the tile. Smooth the rough-cut edges with an abrasive stone or a file.

Cutting holes. To cut a hole with a carbide-tipped hole saw, fasten the tile, glazed side down, to a plank by driving nails partway in on each side (*left*). Cut slowly, using firm but not heavy pressure. To fit the tile around a pipe you cannot remove, cut it in two through the middle of the hole. To cut a hole with nippers, outline the hole on the face of the tile, cut the tile through the center of the outline and use the nippers to nibble out the marked area. When the pieces are installed, only a hairline will show between them.

Setting Separate Tiles

1 Preparing the surface. Spread adhesive—using the kind of adhesive appropriate to your particular surface (*page 22*)—as thinly as possible with the unnotched side of the trowel. Avoid covering reference lines. Let this "skim coat" dry.

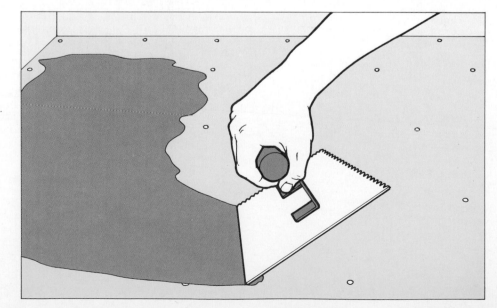

2 Applying adhesive. Spread adhesive over an area of about 10 square feet with the notched edge of the trowel, holding the edge against the surface at a 45° angle. Use only about a cup of adhesive at a time so that adhesive flows freely from the notches. Avoid covering reference lines.

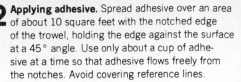

3 Setting tiles. Start setting tiles at reference lines (*right*) near the middle of the room and work toward walls. Press each tile in place with your fingertips, twisting it slightly to set it into the adhesive; do not slide tiles into place or adhesive will fill the grout joint and make grouting impossible. When setting thick tiles with indentations on the backs, apply adhesive also to the back of each tile. Butt the spacing lugs on the edges of the tiles tightly together for a proper fit. Check alignment frequently with a straightedge. If a course is out of line, it can be corrected by opening the joints slightly.

Cut each border tile individually as you reach the end of a course, since border spaces may vary slightly. Remove adhesive from the faces of the tiles with the solvent recommended by the adhesive manufacturer.

4 Beating in the tile. Pad a scrap of 2-by-4 the length of three tiles with several layers of cloth. Put this beater, padded side down, on the set tiles and tap it gently with a hammer several times along its length. Beating in sets the tiles more firmly into the adhesive and helps to ensure a level floor. Let the adhesive harden for 24 hours before grouting. If you must walk on newly laid tile, cover it first with plywood.

Setting Sheets of Tile

Pregrouted tile. Some tile comes in sheets several tiles square, the tiles attached to one another with flexible grout. Set sheets of pregrouted tile, using the techniques shown for individual tiles (*pages 24-25, Steps 1-4*). If one or more tiles in a sheet must be cut to fit around pipes or fixtures, cut the affected tiles out of the sheet with a razor blade and trim away the cut grouting. Set the remaining tiles in the sheet, then cut the detached tiles to fit around the obstacle (*page 24*). Set the cut tiles and, after 24 hours, regrout around them with silicone grouting (*page 27*).

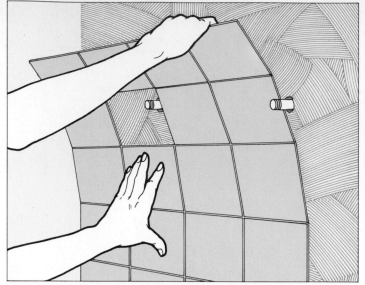

Mosaic tile sheets. Most mosaic tile comes in sheets held together not by grout but by paper on the face of the tiles or by mesh on the back. Roll up the sheet with the back of the tile on the outside. After troweling on adhesive, place the free edge of the sheet where it is to be set and gradually unroll the sheet, pressing the tiles gently into the adhesive. Do not slide sheets into place. Space sheets the same distance apart as the tiles in the sheets. The mesh on mesh-mounted tiles remains in place under the tiles; the paper on paper-faced tiles is removed after the tiles are set by dampening it and peeling it off.

When mosaic tiles must be cut to fit a space, cut the affected tiles out of the sheet, trim them as necessary and set them individually.

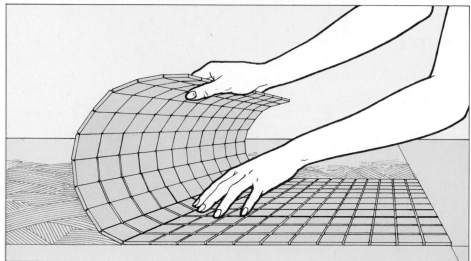

Finishing Techniques

Grouting. Mix grout to the consistency specified on the label. Trowel it into the joints and spread it with a window-washing squeegee or stiff cardboard. After about 15 minutes, wipe up excess grout with a damp sponge, rinsing the sponge frequently. When all grout has been removed, let the tiles dry; polish with a soft cloth.

Applying silicone grouting. Use a caulking gun with the tip cut at a 45° angle to grout between sheets of pregrouted tile with mildew-resistant silicone seal. Fill joints to the same depth as the grouting between tiles. Also grout around any tiles you have set individually. When the silicone is tacky, clean the tiles around the joints, using alcohol on a soft cloth.

Sealing grout. A good way to keep grout joints from becoming discolored by dirt or mildew is to seal them with a penetrating-type liquid sealer after the grout has cured for 28 days. On walls, apply the sealer to the grout joints with a small brush such as a watercolor brush. On floors, spread the sealer over the joints and wipe up any excess with a soft cloth.

Making Minor Repairs

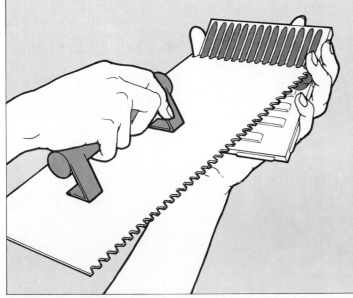

Patching small areas. To replace broken tiles or reset loose tiles, remove tiles from the damaged area, apply adhesive and set the tiles as on pages 24-25. If cramped working space makes applying adhesive to the surface difficult, spread it on the backs of the tiles. If replacement tiles or tiles being reset do not have built-in spacing lugs, space the tiles with toothpicks.

Repairing grout lines. Use an awl to pick out damaged or discolored grout. Mix a little grout, matching the old color as closely as possible, and wipe it into the joint with your finger. A pencil eraser or the butt end of an old toothbrush may be helpful in forcing grout into the joint. Pack the joint tightly, then wipe away any excess and polish the tiles.

Accessories for Bathroom Walls

The essential bathroom accessories—soap dishes, towel bars and toilet-tissue holders—and many less essential ones are available in three types. Flush-set accessories mount on the wall much like tile or paneling; they are installed at the time the wall covering is applied. Recessed accessories, applied at the same stage of wall finishing, are, as the name suggests, fitted into holes in the wall. The third type, surface-mounted accessories, can be installed at any time over the wall covering; some are merely glued on, but the ones held by screws and mounting clips are generally sturdier. The method of fastening the accessory to the clip depends on whether the accessory is ceramic or metal *(right)*.

Vertical or L-shaped grab bars, resembling towel racks but more sturdily mounted, are a useful addition to any bathroom. Like other surface-mounted accessories, they are fixed on top of the wall covering. But plastic anchors should not be used to hold the mounting screws for a grab bar. Some people use hollow-wall fasteners, but it is better to screw a grab bar directly into wood blocking placed behind the wall at the time of framing *(pages 101-102)*.

If a wall is being tiled, flush-set accessories are generally installed. Leave an opening for them at the time of tiling, cutting tiles as needed to trim the edges of the space. When setting or replacing a flush-set accessory, use plaster of paris rather than tile adhesive to bond it to the wall. The plaster grips every little crevice around the opening and expands slightly as it sets, strengthening the bond.

Recessed accessories can be installed in any wall that can be cut, and are suitable for tiled walls if a space for them is planned and the underlying material is cut before tiling. The small opening in the wall must be cut to the same dimensions as the accessory's recessed part, the edges at least 1½ inches from a stud.

Surface-mounted pieces

Drilling tile. Locate accessories so that their screw holes are as near to the centers of tiles as possible. Use rubber cement to stick a piece of thin paperboard, such as a file card, where the accessory is to be fastened. Hold the mounting clip for the accessory against the card and mark the screw holes. Drill with a masonry bit and a variable-speed drill at low speed; apply light pressure to avoid breaking the tile. After the holes are drilled, peel the paperboard from the wall.

Installing ceramic accessories. Screw the metal mounting clip into plastic wall anchors, setting it with its thickest end up. Slide the accessory down over the wedge-shaped clip until it fits snugly against the wall. Grout the joint between the accessory and the wall.

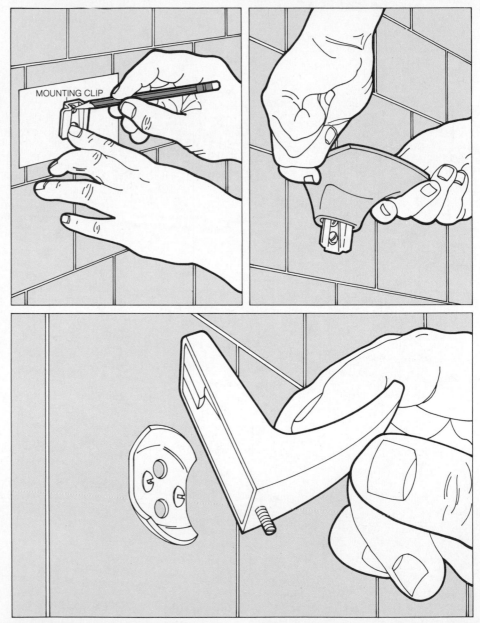

MOUNTING CLIP

Installing metal accessories. Attach the clip to the wall as shown above, with its angled parts at top and bottom. Place the setscrew in the bottom of the accessory. Slip the top of the accessory over the top angle of the mounting clip and drop the bottom of the accessory over the bottom of the clip. Tighten the setscrew against the bottom of the clip with a small screwdriver.

Flush-set accessories

Mixing the plaster of paris. Add water slowly to a pound of plaster of paris in a mixing bowl, stirring constantly. Mix just until the material holds its shape and peaks in the bowl like stiffly beaten egg whites. Avoid excessive stirring; too much air in the mixture will speed setting time. Trowel about a ¼-inch layer onto the back of the accessory, slightly thinner toward the edges.

Setting the accessory. Press the accessory firmly against the wall while wiggling it to force the plaster of paris into irregularities around and behind the adjacent tiles. Wipe off plaster that oozes out the sides of the front flange. Hold the accessory in place until the plaster stiffens, usually a minute or two. The next day, grout around the flange.

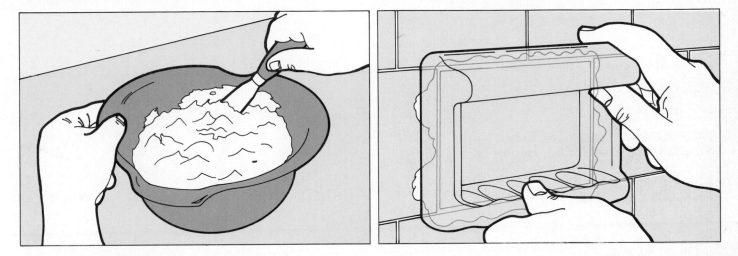

Recessed accessories

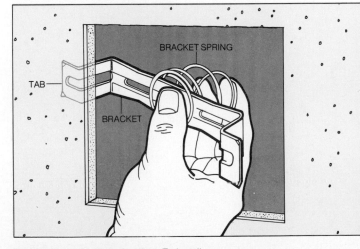

Positioning the hanger bracket. To install a recessed accessory that was planned before the wall was surfaced, screw it directly into wood blocking (*pages 101-102*). For installation after the wall is surfaced, cut and finish the opening, then use a winged bracket to secure the accessory behind the wall (*above*). Slip the first coil of the bracket spring over the center of the bracket with the remainder of the spring pointing away from the spread tabs. Angle the bracket into the recess, spring first, and position its tabs against the back of the wall surface. The spring, pushing against the far side of the wall section, will hold the bracket in place.

Mounting the accessory. Place a bead of colorless caulking compound around the back of the front flange on the accessory. Insert the accessory into its opening. Put one of the mounting screws through the accessory and engage it in the slot in the mounting bracket. Tighten the screw a turn or two. Do the same with the other screw and then tighten both of the screws to hold the accessory in place.

Plastic Laminates: Easy to Mount and Maintain

Plastic laminate—the tough, impermeable, stain-resistant material that now is almost universal for kitchen countertops—also makes attractive covering for kitchen and bathroom walls, tables, vanities and cabinet doors. Applying laminate sheets is almost as easy as painting and generally far more satisfactory for surfaces subject to heavy wear.

Most laminates used on surfaces other than walls come in sheets 4 by 8 feet in size and 1/16 inch thick; walls *(pages 33-35)* require only 1/32-inch material. The sheets expand and contract with changes in temperature and humidity and should be allowed to adapt to the room where they will be used—stack them loosely against a wall for 48 hours.

Laminates can be applied over plywood, particle board, hardboard or old laminate. However, it is all but impossible to apply laminate over ceramic tile or linoleum; such surfaces must first be covered with underlayment to which the laminate is then cemented. Two types of contact adhesive are widely used. One, based on water, is nonflammable and nontoxic but lower in bonding strength than the second type, which contains a petroleum-based solvent, highly flamma-

ble and toxic. If you must use this type indoors, keep it away from heat, sparks and open flames. Do not smoke while working, extinguish pilot lights and gas burners, open the circuit breakers controlling all nearby stoves, heaters and electric motors—including fans and refrigerators—and provide cross ventilation in the work area.

Because of the hazards of petroleum-based adhesive—and because of the difficulty of handling large sheets of laminate in small rooms—work outdoors as much as possible. Moderate temperatures are necessary; contact adhesives dry tediously slowly at temperatures much below 70° and at higher temperatures dry too fast and lose bonding strength.

Applying laminate to countertops or similar surfaces is easiest when the countertop is being built *(page 42)* or has been removed to a roomy work area. But if removing an already installed countertop is impractical, apply laminate with the countertop in place *(page 32)*.

In either case, remove any metal edging from the countertop and the backsplash. You can later cover these edges with laminate for a finished appearance or install new metal edging *(page 32)*.

The latter process is easier for novices and hides minor misalignments of the top surface laminate. Also remove any metal cove molding that may be attached to the ends or back of the countertop.

Before applying laminate to a top surface, remove the sink or other fixtures recessed into cutouts in the surface. All cutouts in new laminate are made after the laminate has been bonded.

Any surface to be laminated should be clean, dry and even, with protrusions sanded down and holes filled with wood putty. If you apply new laminate directly over the old, flatten bubbles by breaking them with a hammer and sanding them down, or by countersinking a flathead wood screw through the bubble into the base. Cement loose edges and sand the whole surface thoroughly before applying adhesive; sand, sawdust or laminate chips left on the countertop can make permanent lumps in the finished surface.

Cover the front of a cabinet door in the same way as a countertop but be sure to cover the back of the door with a thinner backing laminate. It will keep the door from shrinking or swelling unevenly with changes in humidity, thus loosening the bond of the adhesive on the front.

Covering a Countertop

1 Cutting laminate. Mark the pieces to be cut out of each laminate sheet 1/4 inch larger in all dimensions than the surfaces to be covered, to provide a margin for error. When laminating a countertop that has been removed from its counter, plan to remove the backsplash and cover the whole top surface *(Step 4)*. For a countertop being laminated in place with the backsplash attached, cover the top surface up to the bottom edge of the backsplash. Place the marked sheet face up on a firm support or the floor, and score the sheet with a blade called a laminate scriber. Then bend the edge of the sheet *(right)* until it snaps like glass along the scored line. You can also cut the sheet with a saber saw using a fine-toothed blade, but test the blade on a scrape of laminate first to make sure it will not cause excessive chipping.

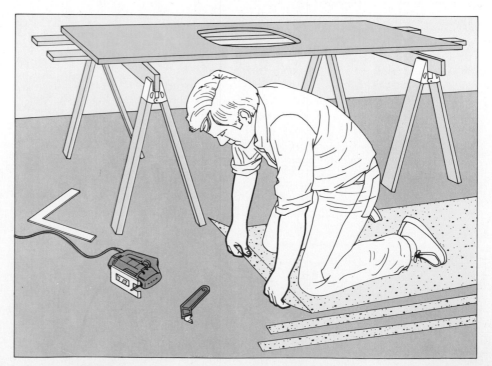

2 **Putting on edge strips.** Attach edge strips first at the short sides of the countertop. If you are laminating a U-shaped countertop, begin at the bottom of the U. If you plan to use metal edging, see instructions on page 32. Apply adhesive to both laminate and edge with a brush or a narrow paint roller, using only a little at a time. When the adhesive has dried, hold an edge strip between thumbs and forefingers *(right);* position it as accurately as possible and set it in place. Once in contact, it cannot be shifted. Tap the surface with a hammer and wood block.

To bend laminate around a gentle curve, soak it in hot water until it becomes flexible, wipe it dry and attach it before it cools.

3 **Trimming projections.** Wearing a mask and goggles, trim off laminate projecting at the top, bottom and sides of the edges with a plane, a router fitted with a carbide trimming bit *(right)* or a special laminate trimmer rented from your supplier. Many installers trim the short edges before laminating the long edges so that the long strip laps over the ends of the short ones.

4 **Bonding a top surface.** Apply adhesive to the top surface and the laminate, using a little extra adhesive around the edges of both. When the adhesive is dry, lay pieces of lumber ¾ inch thick at 1-foot intervals across the top surface. Lay the laminate face up on the wood supports and aligned with the top surface. Slide out one end support and press that end of the laminate sheet down. Remove remaining supports one at a time, pressing down laminate as you work toward the other end of the surface.

Tap the surface with a wood block and a hammer. Trim off the projecting edges as in Step 3, but coat the edging below with petroleum jelly to prevent scorching by the router or laminate trimmer. Bevel the sharp edges of laminate along the top and at corners, using a file or a router with a bevel cutter.

5 **Making cutouts.** Cut out holes for sinks, plumbing and electrical outlets after attaching laminate. If you are relaminating an old surface that already has cutouts, drill a 1-inch hole inside the line of each cutout and cut the laminate with a router, following the rim of the original hole. If you have made an entirely new countertop, mark each hole as shown on page 43. Drill a ¼-inch starter hole—and a pilot hole at each corner for cuts with corners—and cut out the opening with a saber saw fitted with a metal-cutting blade. Smooth the edges of the cutout with a router, a laminate cutter or a file.

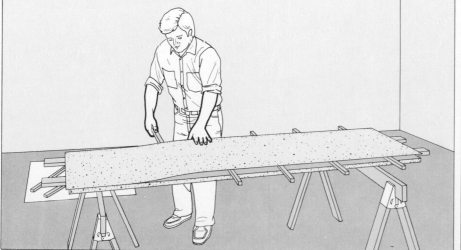

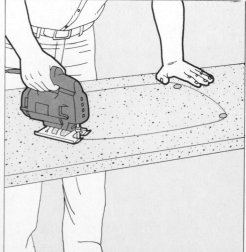

Edging a Backsplash in Place

Covering the backsplash. When laminating the backsplash of a countertop that has not been detached from the counter, apply laminate first to the front of the backsplash and trim the top edge flush with a sanding block. Apply a strip cut as accurately as possible to the top edge of the backsplash (*right*).

If you are covering a countertop detached from the counter, cover the backsplash as you did the other surfaces—bonding first the sides, then the front and finally the top. Reattach the backsplash after lamination as on page 45, Step 8, putting a bead of silicone seal along the bottom edge of the backsplash to seal the joint.

With the countertop in place, caulk between the top edge of the backsplash and the wall as needed. If there is no backsplash, seal the wall edges of the countertops as shown at lower right.

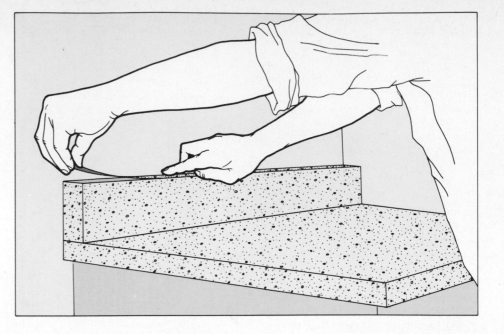

Finishing Edges with Metal

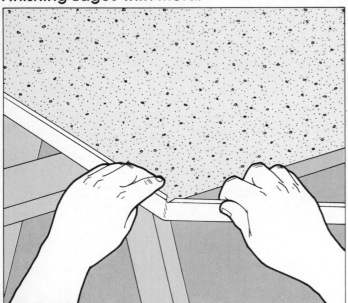

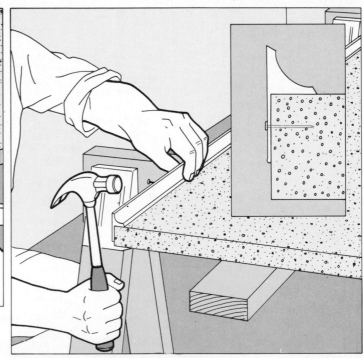

Adding a snap-on edge. If you laminate only the top surface of a countertop, finish the edges with C-shaped metal molding. To allow for error, cut a strip a little longer than the edge it will cover. Slip one end of the strip over the edge where it meets a wall. If the countertop is slightly too thick, trim off the bottom of the countertop around the edge with a router. Secure the molding end with a brad through its bottom lip. Snap the molding onto the countertop edge.

At each outside corner cut a wedge of 10° or so out of the top and bottom lips of the molding and bend the molding around the corner. At inside corners, miter the ends of two strips. Secure the molding with brads through its lower lip.

Adding metal cove molding. If, instead of having a backsplash, a countertop adjoins a wall or walls covered with laminate, ceramic tile or other waterproof material, seal the joint between countertop and wall. If the countertop is detached from its counter, before installing it fasten metal cove molding to the wall edges of the countertop by nailing through the flange at the back of the molding (*inset*). Run a bead of silicone seal along the back of the molding, then install the countertop. If the countertop has not been detached, simply caulk along the joint.

Paneling Walls

Plastic laminate for walls comes factory-bonded to an underlayment of rigid plastic or hardboard. The panels are about ⅛ inch thick and come in 4-by-8-foot sheets or in tub-enclosure kits that usually include a piece about 5 feet wide and two strips about 30 inches wide.

Laminate panels can be mounted on almost any clean, smooth surface, including plastic, wallboard or tile. Wallpaper or vinyl wall covering should be removed, however, and painted surfaces should be scraped and sanded.

If a tub wall is in poor condition, cut away a strip of wall covering 6 inches wide above the tub rim and nail exterior-grade plywood to the exposed studs.

Cut panels as for countertops *(pages 42-45)*, leaving them ⅛ inch short in each dimension to provide expansion space. Metal or vinyl molding *(right)*, shaped for use in corners, on tub rims and on walls, fills and seals joints.

Panel edging should extend only about halfway into the grooves of these moldings. If necessary, bevel the panel edge along the back to let it fit easily. Never nail into the panel.

Wherever the horizontal molding meets the vertical molding, as when installing wainscoting *(page 34)*, you should trim or miter the ends of molding strips to make a smooth fit.

Trim and fit all panels carefully before applying adhesive to the wall and the panel; you will usually have only a tiny margin for error. Make all cutouts beforehand; a paper template of wall fixtures *(page 34)* is a useful guide for establishing the location of cutouts on the panels that will cover these fixtures.

Most panel adhesives are highly flammable. Handle adhesives with the same care as other laminate adhesives *(page 30)*, and keep the room well ventilated. Follow the manufacturer's instructions on adhesive application and drying time. Some panel adhesives bond instantly, requiring great skill in aligning panels; others bond more slowly, allowing time for adjustments. A properly applied adhesive provides a watertight bond between wall and panel, but be sure to apply a silicone seal along the expansion space at the tops and bottoms of panels for complete moisture protection.

The Families of Molding

One-piece molding. Cut from long strips of metal or plastic, one-piece molding is usually installed a length at a time with the laminate panels *(page 34)*. Shown below are: tub-rim and tub-bend moldings *(page 35)*, used along the straight and curved edges of the tub; inside and outside corner moldings that accommodate single panels or two panels that meet at a corner; double-flanged division molding to cover seams between adjoining panels on the same wall; and edge molding, also used as cap molding along the tops of panels in wainscot installations.

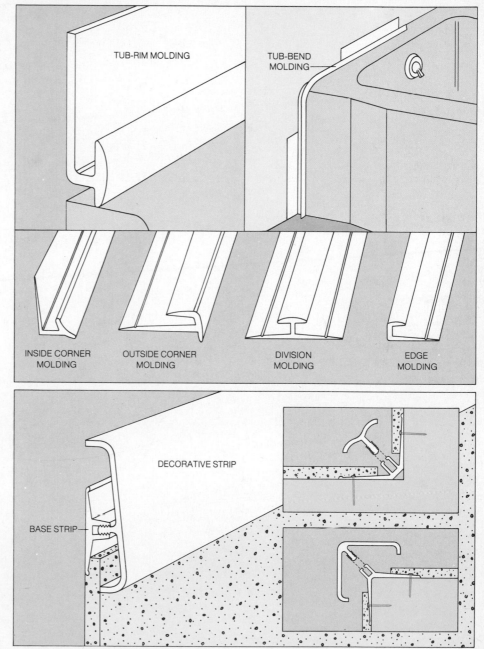

Two-piece molding. In this system a molding such as the cap above utilizes a base strip, mounted with nails or adhesive before paneling, and a decorative outer strip. This strip snaps into the base after paneling as shown in the exploded cross sections of an inside corner *(top inset)* and an outside corner *(bottom inset)*.

Putting Up the Panels

1 Installing molding. Remove baseboards, ceiling molding and wall fixtures. On tiled walls attach molding strips with panel adhesive; on plaster or wallboard walls, nail them to studs where possible and countersink the nailheads. Use a plumb line to get division strips vertical. If you use two-piece molding for floor-to-ceiling paneling, attach all the base strips before mounting the panels; if you use one-piece molding, attach only a single strip in the corner.

For wainscot installations, draw a horizontal guideline at the desired height on the wall or walls to be paneled. Mount vertical molding as for full-wall installations. If you use two-piece molding, cover the top edges of the panels, after the panels have been mounted, with cap molding *(page 33)*. If you use one-piece molding, fit the top edges into edge molding fastened to the wall before panels are mounted *(right)*. Where edge molding meets vertical molding, cut away flanges of the edge molding *(top inset)* for a smooth fit of moldings and panels *(bottom inset)*.

2 Making cutouts. Where cutouts will be required, make a template by taping heavy paper over that part of the wall. Mark on the paper the exact dimensions of the panel that will be mounted over that area. Carefully poke holes through the paper to mark the locations of pipes, electrical outlets or recessed cabinets. Remove the template and tape it to the face of the panel. Mark the outlines of the cutouts on the panel, then place the panel face up before cutting out the openings with a saber saw.

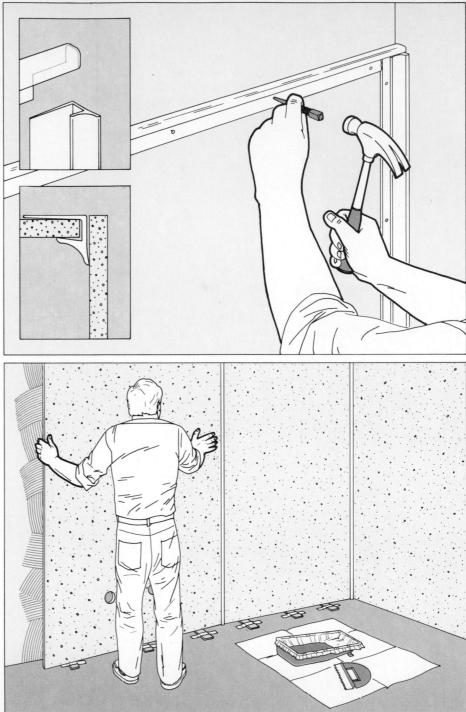

3 Mounting panels. Place cardboard shims about 1⁄16 inch thick on the floor along the wall. If you are using two-piece molding, apply adhesive to the wall and to the back of the panel with a notched spreader, covering the flanges but not the grooves of molding. When the adhesive dries to the consistency recommended by the manufacturer, mount the panel on the wall *(above)*. Apply pressure over the whole surface with a hammer and a wood block. Tap the decorative strips into the base strips. When the in-

stallation is complete, remove the shims from the panel bottoms and then cement vinyl cove molding along the base of the wall.

For one-piece molding, begin paneling in the corner where the molding is in place. Cut and fit a panel, and fit a strip of molding onto its outside edge. Mount the panel, sliding its inside edge into the groove of the corner molding. Continue around the room, similarly mounting panels and molding so that you finish at the starting point.

4 **Door and window treatments.** Mount a strip of edge molding as close to the door or window casing as possible and fit one end of the panel into it. To fit panel edges under window aprons and stools, carefully scribe *(page 71)* and cut the panel to fit around the trim.

If you prefer not to use molding, you can remove the wood casings of the door or window and, using a router, make rabbets an inch wide and ⅛ inch deep along the wall edges. Mount panels so that they will extend slightly less than an inch into the rabbet, then remount the casings over the panel edges. Rabbeting can also be used to fit panel edges under window aprons and stools.

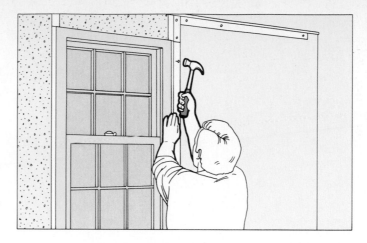

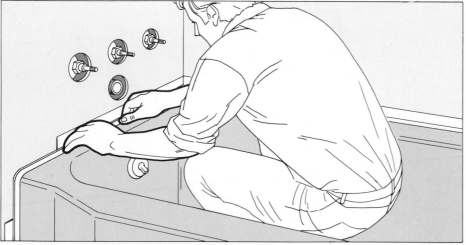

Finishing around a Tub

1 **Mounting the molding.** Measure and cut all molding strips as for other wall installations. If you use two panels on the back wall, plumb a line at the midpoint for the divider molding.

If you use one-piece molding, nail on one vertical corner strip. Caulk all around the tub rim where it meets the wall, then nail tub-rim molding along the rim of the tub and tub-bend molding around the curved shoulder of the tub where it meets an end wall. If you use two-piece molding, tape shims ¹⁄₁₆ inch thick along the wall rim of the tub.

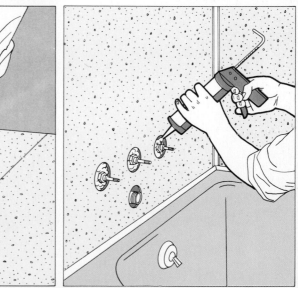

2 **Mounting the panels.** Cut and fit the panels, make cutouts for fixtures, and mount panels in the same manner as other wall installations. If you use one-piece molding, be sure to fill the grooves in the tub-rim and tub-bend molding with beads of sealant before mounting the panels inside the tub enclosure. To cut an end wall panel to fit precisely the curvature of a tub shoulder, measure and mark on the face of the panel the dimensions of the corner to be cut out. Then bend a piece of wire solder around the curve of the tub shoulder, transfer this curve to the panel markings by tracing the bent solder *(above),* and cut out the corner.

3 **Sealing the panels.** Remove shims from the tub rim and clean the joint with mineral spirits. Squeeze a bead of sealant into the joint and smooth it with a finger. Repeat the sealing process along the ceiling joint. Use a caulking gun to fill the fixture openings *(above)* before reattaching the fixtures.

Synthetic Marble: Luxurious and Stainproof

Marble walls, vanity tops and countertops give a luxurious look to a kitchen or a bathroom, but cutting and installing the fragile stone calls for special tools and professional expertise. Moreover, real marble is easily stained by foodstuffs, cosmetics and forgotten cigarettes.

A more practical and less expensive way to achieve the marble look is with synthetic marble. One type, called cultured marble, consists of finely ground marble chips embedded in plastic and covered with a gel coating. Like real marble, it requires professional cutting, but countertops and paneling are available in presized, one-piece units. Its marble-like color and veining, unfortunately, are only skin-deep; subsurface cuts and scratches in it cannot be satisfactorily repaired.

A second type, sold under the trade name Corian, is a mineral-filled acrylic plastic that also looks like the real thing. Its color and patterns go all the way through the sheets and it is usually preferred by amateurs since it can be cut, drilled, routed and sanded with woodworking tools, although carbide-tipped cutting edges are recommended. The illustrations that follow apply particularly to this material.

The acrylic synthetic is available in sheets 30 inches wide and up to 10 feet long, and also in one-piece, precut sink-countertop units and in precut kits for tub and shower enclosures. Three thicknesses are available: ¼ inch for paneling walls—including tub and shower enclosures *(pages 38-39)*—and ½ and ¾ inch for vanity tops and countertops. The material is heavy; a countertop ¾ inch thick weighs as much as 14 pounds per linear foot. Make sure that the cabinets supporting such a countertop are sturdy; strengthen the framing if necessary.

Because the synthetic marble is more expensive than ceramic tile or plastic laminate, its use in bathrooms is generally limited to paneling around a bathtub or a shower enclosure, either as wainscoting or as full-wall panels.

A typical kit for paneling an enclosure with acrylic material includes four ¼-inch panels 30 by 57 inches plus a filler panel 10 by 57 inches to cover any gap between the panels on back walls more than 60 inches wide. Trim strips *(page 39)* come with some kits or can be cut in 2-inch widths from ½- or ¾-inch panels; they are used along the top and side edges of wall panels to give a finished, framed effect. They can also be used in corners or around tub rims to conceal cutting errors and to cover gaps caused by out-of-plumb walls. At the tops of full-wall panels, use ¾-inch trim set ½ inch below ceiling level to conceal gaps caused by faulty cutting or an irregular ceiling.

Before paneling a wall with any synthetic marble material, remove wallpaper. If you are replacing a damaged bathroom wall or putting in a new one, cover the existing wallboard or masonry with waterproof dry wall *(page 103)*. Remove floor molding where necessary and remove all wall fixtures, recessed or protruding, located in places that the panels will cover. Using a paper template *(page 34, Step 2)*, locate the positions of these fixtures on the panels. Before attaching the panels, provide cutouts for the fixtures, using the method shown on page 37 for acrylic. Before applying the panels over tile, clean the tiles with a strong household detergent and sand them with coarse sandpaper.

Synthetic marble is attached to walls and countertops with a neoprene-base adhesive, available from dealers, that is applied with a caulking gun. The adhesive is highly flammable; handle it as carefully as you would a plastic laminate adhesive *(page 30)*, observing the same safety precautions.

Installing Countertops and Vanity Tops

Cutting acrylic resin sheets. Wear goggles and a respirator and keep the room ventilated while cutting. Lay 2-by-4s or other scrap lumber across sawhorses. Lay the sheet face up on the 2-by-4s. Clamp a straightedge to the sheet as a guide for the saw, and place wide strips of masking tape on either side of the cut line to minimize scratching. Set the saw blade to cut ¼ inch deeper than the sheets; the blade will notch the supports but not sever them.

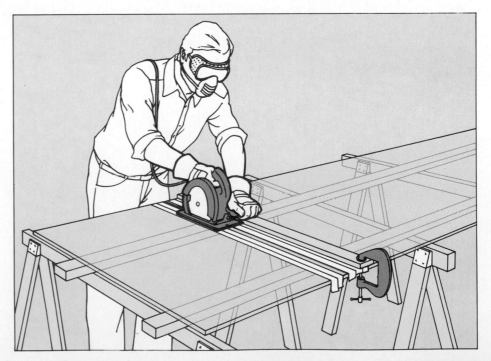

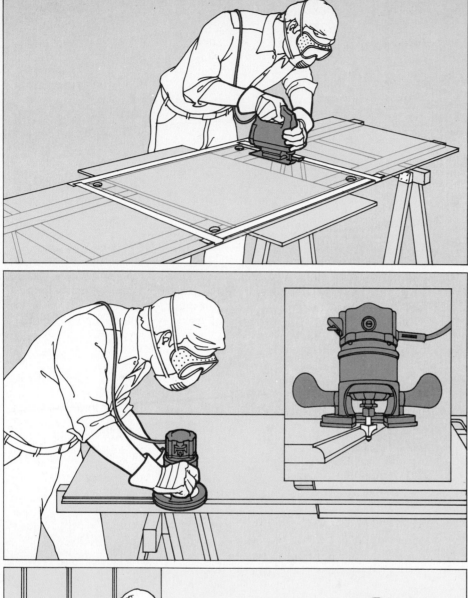

Making cutouts. Measure and mark cutouts. Use a hole saw to cut a 1-inch-diameter hole at each corner of each cutout; square corners create stress points and may cause the sheet to crack. Cut two facing edges of the cutout with a saber saw, then slide a thin board under the cutout to support the cutout piece as the remaining cuts are made. Sand the edges smooth. When installing a cook top, line the cutout edges with reflective aluminum tape 2 inches wide.

Finishing edges. Before fixing the sheet to the cabinets or installing sinks or cook tops, round off all exposed edges and corners by sanding or by decoratively carving with a router. Wipe any grit off the router base and the surface of the sheet to avoid surface scratches. Use a carbide-tipped bit with a ball-bearing guide (*inset*). Move the router counterclockwise around outer edges to prevent chipping. Make an initial pass to remove most of the edge material and a second pass to finish the edge.

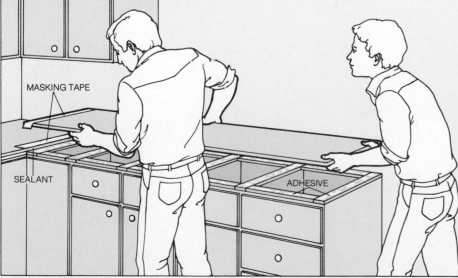

MASKING TAPE

SEALANT

ADHESIVE

Installing and joining sheets. Level and shim cabinets as necessary (*page 48*). When installing a one-piece countertop, place 1-inch beads of neoprene adhesive at 6-inch intervals around the top edges of the cabinet framing and press the counter firmly into the adhesive within 5 minutes.

When assembling two or more sheets into an L-shaped or a U-shaped countertop, set the longest section in place first. Run a continuous bead of silicone sealant along one of the edges to be joined. Cover the tops of both sheets adjacent to the joint with strips of masking tape. Jam the second sheet tight against the first, squeezing excess sealant out onto the masking tape. Smooth the joint with a damp cloth, remove the tape and let the joint set overnight. Then smooth the joint with fine sandpaper.

Attaching backsplashes. Run a continuous bead of silicone sealant along the bottom edge of the backsplash and press the strip into position at the back edge of the countertop. Butt-join the splash strips with sealant. Wipe up the excess with a damp cloth and let the joints cure.

Instead of installing a backsplash, you can panel the wall behind the countertop with ¼-inch acrylic resin paneling. The panel should extend several inches below the surface of the countertop. Seal the joint between the countertop and the panel with silicone sealant.

Hanging a sink. Use standard hardware to install self-rimmed sinks (*page 122*) and inserts supported by stainless-steel rims (*page 43*); tighten mounting screws lightly to avoid cracking the sheet. Dealers supply special mounting assemblies (*inset*) for underhung vanity sinks. Place the bracket on the sink rim (*below*) and mark the underside of the vanity top through the adjustment slot. Drill six ¼-inch pilot holes, slightly deeper than the threaded brass screw anchors supplied with the assembly, at equal intervals around the rim. Tap in the anchors and attach the brackets with mounting screws.

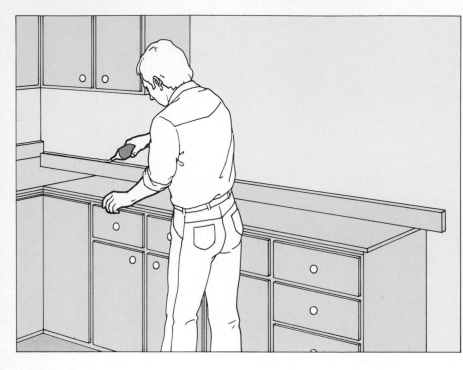

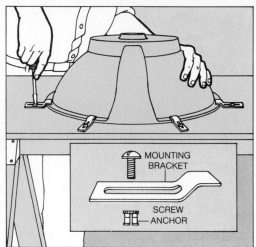

Paneling a Tub or Shower Enclosure

1 **Preparing for installation.** Using a level, draw a horizontal line around the enclosure at the desired panel height. Use a plumb line to draw vertical lines on the walls 2 inches in from the outside edge of the tub. Drive tenpenny nails partway into the wall at 1-foot intervals around the tub rim. The nails will act as shims for the panels to rest on when they are installed; space will be left for caulking when they are removed.

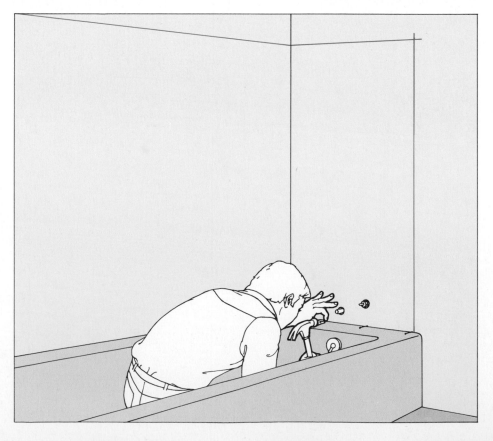

2 Attaching the panels. Measure and cut the panels, setting each in place atop the nails driven in around the tub edge to check the fit. Install the back-wall panels first, then the end-wall panels. In each case, use a caulking gun to run a ¼-inch bead of adhesive around the space the panel will cover: ½ inch in from the top, bottom and side edges, one third of the way in from the side edges, and around fixture holes (inset). Keep the bead rounded; do not press the caulking gun's nozzle against the wall.

With a helper, set each panel in place, press it firmly against the wall, then pull it away for 30 seconds (right). Press it back in place and apply hand pressure over the whole panel surface. Butt the inner edges of the end-wall panels against the sides of the back-wall panels.

3 Attaching the filler panel. Measure and cut a ¼-inch panel to cover the space between the two back-wall panels. Locate the filler panel at the center of the back wall and mark guidelines on the two back-wall panels. Apply caulking just inside the guidelines and adhesive along the back-wall panel edges. Press the filler panel into place in a single operation instead of attaching, removing and reattaching as you did with the back-wall panels. Wipe away the excess caulking with a damp sponge.

For full-wall panels use a ½-inch filler strip to match the ¾-inch trim strips you will apply later.

ADHESIVE   CAULK

4 Applying trim strips. Cut a trim strip (½ inch for wainscoting, ¾ inch for a full wall) the length of the back wall and attach it to the wall with adhesive directly above the panels. Caulk any gaps between the trim strip and the tops of the panels. Similarly apply top trim strips to the end walls, cut flush with the outer edges of the panels. Install the vertical trim strips to cover the outer edges of the panels and the ends of the top trim strips. Transfer the line of the curve from the edge of the tub to the strip as shown on page 23, or use a compass to scribe the curve (page 71, Step 2). Measure and mark the strip for length by holding it in position with the curved end shimmed away from the tub rim by a tenpenny nail. Cut, sand and install the strip.

Let the adhesive cure overnight, remove the shim nails and caulk the joints. Caulk around the cutouts. Let the caulk cure for six hours.

Carpentry for Convenience

Truing a cabinet. **Truing a cabinet.** The carpenter's level and shims seen atop this kitchen cabinet are needed to install it properly. Because floors and walls are seldom exactly flat surfaces, each cabinet must be adjusted with thin wood shim strips to push it forward or upward to align it with the others. Only when the cabinets are true—that is, perfectly horizontal and vertical—are they screwed to walls and each other *(pages 46-48)*.

The tools of the carpenter—hammers, saws, hand drills and the rest—can work wonders in a bathroom or a kitchen. Superficially, these rooms are places of ceramics, chrome and plastic, where wood is seldom seen—yet with nothing more than basic woodworking tools and without ever touching plumbing, you can add to storage capacity, increase efficiency and improve appearance.

Carpentry in these rooms, however, calls for special care. Both are generally small places, crowded and short of working space, and both are likely to contain coverings on walls, floors and countertops that, while resistant to moisture and chemicals, are brittle and easily cracked. You must often create an assembly area outside a room, and when you work inside, protect surfaces with newspapers. The trick is to analyze a job beforehand, separating inside from outside work.

Installing cabinets *(pages 46-49)* is inside work, of course: the units come ready-made, and the jobs of mounting them and linking them into a single braced structure must be done on the walls and floors they occupy. But adding a fitted top to a set of base cabinets is something that can be done outside almost entirely. If you do not have a large kitchen like the one shown on pages 42-45, use your workshop or if necessary the garage to cut a core for the countertop, assemble it and cover it with tile or plastic laminate.

Smaller jobs, in which minor changes have the effect of major improvements, make easy inside work—a hard-to-reach corner houses a Lazy Susan, a spare cabinet gets a retractable trash container, horizontal shelving is replaced by vertical dividers to store platters, cookie sheets and pot lids *(pages 50-51)*. Bigger inside jobs will take you into normally hidden areas. You may break into a wall to make recesses for shelves and medicine chests, or make openings in walls, floors and ceilings for electrical wiring and the ducts of a kitchen range hood. In each case you must cut off electrical circuits in the room and may have to disturb older ducts and existing plumbing. For these jobs, clear the room of obstructions and close it off.

Improvements in the appearance of a room usually lend themselves well to a combination of inside and outside work. You can, for instance, update an old-fashioned claw-footed bathtub by boxing it in with moisture-resistant plywood, or convert the same tub into what looks like a sunken model by building a rim-level platform with steps leading up to it—and for both jobs, you can make the big pieces for the assembly outside the bathroom. The most luxurious addition of all is such a job. The dry-heat bath called a sauna *(pages 64-68)* was once as rare—and almost as expensive—as a private swimming pool. Today, a home carpenter with 9 feet of space can put one together in a weekend—then relax in steamy splendor.

A Custom-made Counter for a Ready-made Base

The standard countertop is essentially a long board 1½ inches thick and about 25 inches deep. A vertical backsplash 4 inches high usually runs along the rear edge, and the entire assembly rises about 36 inches above the floor. Many modern countertops have self-rimmed sinks and the units of a cooking range set into them. A flangelike, stainless-steel sink frame may be used to support some sink models and also such inserts as cutting boards and heatproof plates.

A countertop may consist of a solid length of hardwood or of a textured synthetic material. It may also consist of a less expensive material, such as particle board or exterior-grade plywood, cov-ered with a decorative surface such as tile or high-pressure laminated plastic. For the installation of plastic laminates and tiles, see pages 24-27 and 30-32.

As an alternative to such an assembly, you can buy a countertop complete with a backsplash and factory-installed lami-nate. Factory-made tops are easy to in-stall—you need only saw them to length, cut out the openings and screw them to a counter—but they have their drawbacks, especially on L-shaped counters. Because the backsplash is already in place, a ready-made must be miter cut at the an-gle of the L. Mitered joints are longer and weaker than butt joints and a long mi-tered seam in surface laminate provides a channel through which water can seep, warping or rotting the core below. And the backsplash of a ready-made top can-not be easily fitted to bowed or bumpy walls. When you construct a top from scratch, you can use butt joints, fit the backsplash precisely to the wall and minimize water seepage by locating a 2- or 3-inch laminate seam at the sink cutout, far from the butt joint.

To determine the top's depth measure the distance from the cabinet front to the wall and add 1 inch for overhang. The length depends on the layout of the cabi-nets; set a top over the long leg of an L-shaped layout, and add 1 inch of over-hang for ends that do not abut a wall.

1 **Assembling the core.** With a circular or saber saw cut a core ¾ inch thick to the right length and depth. To join two pieces at right angles, apply white construction glue to the edges, then re-inforce the joint with corrugated steel nails driven across the seam at 1½-inch intervals. Turn the board upside down and hammer a second series of corrugated nails across the back of the seam.

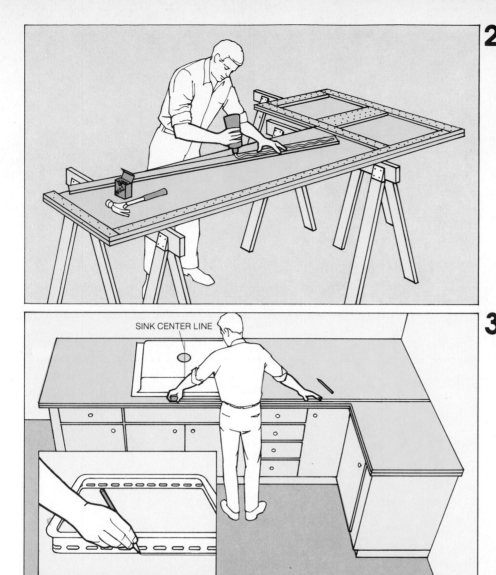

2 Installing the battens. To increase the thickness of the core to 1½ inches, you must add strips called battens, 2 inches wide and ¾ inch thick. Cut the battens from stock to match the sides of the core, butting at the corners; the locations of the butt joints are unimportant, but the strips must cover the perimeter of the core.

Turn the core upside down, apply a ribbon of white construction glue to the wide surface of a batten strip and press the glued batten to the core, with the outside edges of the mated pieces exactly flush. When the glue has set slightly, hammer a zigzag pattern of 1⅛-inch nails, set about 1½ inches apart, through the batten and into the core. Repeat the procedure for all the battens. If the countertop contains a butt joint, cut a batten 6 inches wide to the length of the exposed seam and install it along the joint.

SINK CENTER LINE

3 Positioning a sink. Mark the center on the front edge of the sink cabinet and measure from this mark to the nearest side wall. Set the core on the base cabinets and draw a line across the top of the core from front to rear at the midpoint of the sink cabinet. Mark the center of the sink assembly on the edges of the sink rim, front and rear. Turn the sink upside down, line up the marks with the line on the core and move the sink along this line until the rim is at least 2 inches from the front of the core and 1 inch from the rear. Then trace around the sink's rim.

For a sink supported by a stainless-steel frame (*inset*), center the rim upright on the pencil line and trace the outline. Cutting-board and hot-plate inserts can be positioned almost anywhere on the countertop, as long as they are at least 2 inches from the front and 1 inch from the rear.

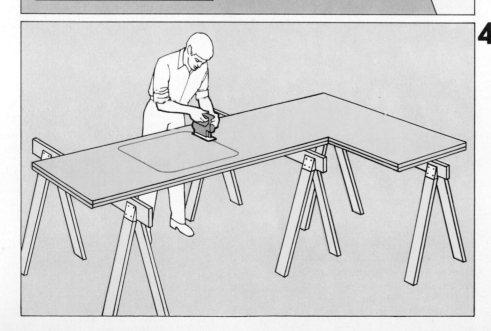

4 Making the sink cutout. Set the sink aside and return the core to the sawhorses. Mark points ¼ inch inside the outline of the sink rim on all four sides and, using a straightedge and soft pencil, connect the marks to outline a sink cutout ¼ inch inside the original. Drill a pilot hole 1 inch inside the outline and, beginning at this hole, cut along the outline with a saber saw to form the sink opening. For a sink-frame cutout, simply drill a pilot hole and cut along the original outline.

To make the splashboard, measure the lengths of the countertop edges that will rest against a wall; where two such edges meet at right angles, subtract ¾ inch from one of the measurements. With a saber or circular saw cut strips of core stock 4 inches wide to your measurements.

At this point apply tiling or a surface laminate to the core, battens and splashboard by the methods shown on pages 24-27 and 30-32.

5 **Installing the backsplash molding.** Cut metal L molding the length of the backsplash; trim the corner of the wide side of the L at a 45° angle. With the backsplash bottom up, set the molding in place with the wide side of the L flat against the bottom of the splash, and fasten it with lath nails at 1-inch intervals. File the rough ends of the molding smooth.

6 **Measuring a bowed wall.** Set the countertop in place on the cabinets, with its rear edges against the walls. If there are gaps along the line where the countertop meets a wall—an indication that the wall may be bowed—measure the space between the countertop and walls at 12-inch intervals and mark the intervals and measurements on the countertop.

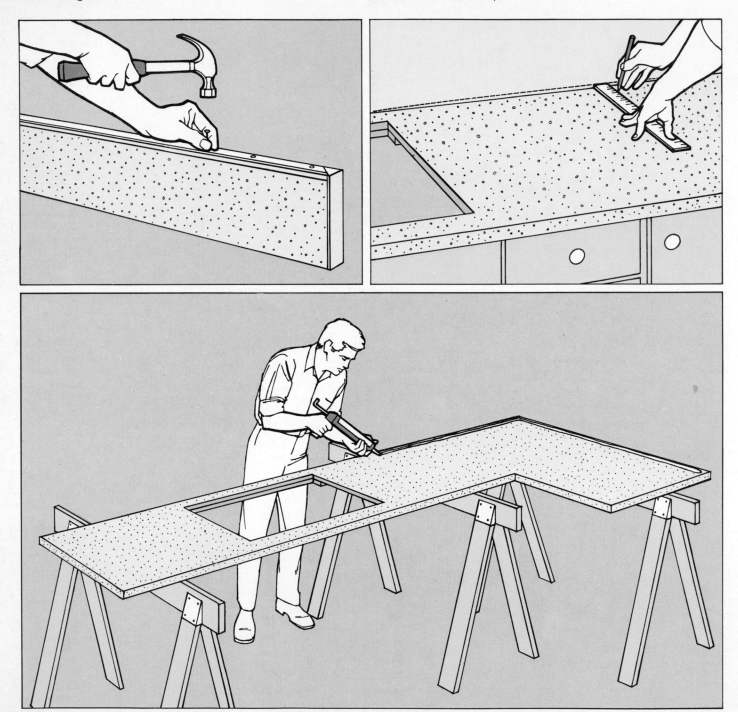

7 **Drilling and caulking for the splashboard.** Return the countertop to the sawhorses and, using a ³⁄₁₆-inch bit, drill a series of holes starting 1 inch in from the end of the countertop. Locate the holes ³⁄₈ inch from the back edge of the countertop and space them 8 inches apart. Run a bead of caulking around the countertop along the line formed by the holes.

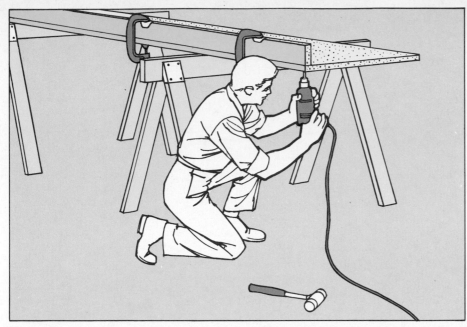

8 **Installing the backsplash.** Secure the backsplash in position with a pair of C clamps and hammer a 2½-inch No. 10 drivescrew into the first predrilled hole and through the backsplash molding. Use a power screwdriver to finish driving the screw. Repeat the procedure at every hole, repositioning the C clamps as necessary. At each gap measurement, tap the backsplash with a mallet until it overlaps the counter edge by a distance equal to the gap, then drive in a screw.

Reading the measurements is easiest if you work from below (*left*); but if that position is awkward, turn the countertop over and screw from above. Caution: Avoid reshaping the backsplash by more than ¼ inch—a sharp curve can cause a screw to break through the backsplash. To join backsplash strips at right angles, drive 1¼-inch nails spaced ¾ inch apart through the back of one strip into the end of the other.

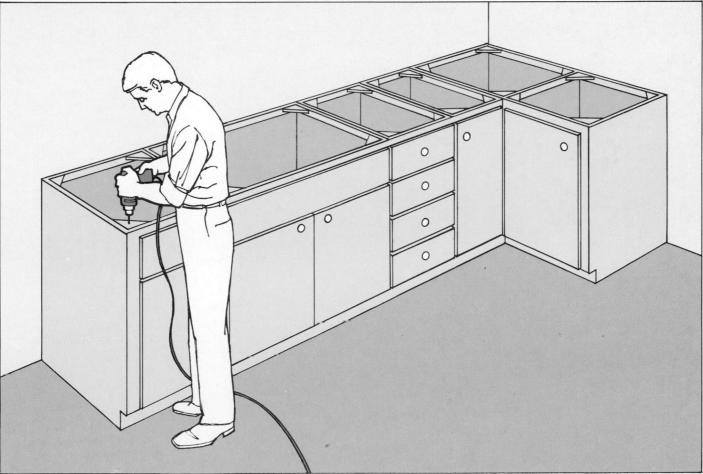

9 **Completing the installation.** Drill ³⁄₁₆-inch holes through the centers of the braces at the outer corners of the end cabinets. Set the countertop in position and, working from below, drive No. 10 screws up through these holes into the battens above. The thickness of the braces will determine the length of the screws, but be careful not to use a screw so long that it extends through the core of the countertop and punctures the tile or laminate surface. Caution: Do not use an adhesive, rather than screws, to anchor the top—prying off a glued countertop for repair or alteration is not only much more difficult than simply withdrawing the screws but also is likely to damage the cabinets and the countertop.

Fitting Cabinets to the Walls and Floors

The decor of a kitchen is set largely by the style and finish of its cabinets. Its efficiency depends largely on their size and placement. But just as important as the cabinets themselves is the care with which they are installed. Poorly installed cabinets will sag from the start; their doors will swing open on their own or refuse to open at all. Bad installation will ruin good cabinets by wearing out their hinges and weakening their structure.

The installation job begins well before you set to work on the cabinets themselves. Unless you are putting new cabinets against an unused wall, you first must remove the old ones. Do not simply pry them off the wall with a crowbar—old cabinets are worth saving for a workroom, darkroom or children's room. Take them down by first removing the screws that fasten cabinets to one another, then the screws that hold the cabinets to the walls. If the slots in the screwheads are too worn to accept a screwdriver, use a power drill to drive a bit down through the head. The head will drop off, and you can pull the cabinets from the wall, then remove the screw shank with pliers.

With the old cabinets out of the way, mark the measurements for the new ones on the walls. Use a level to find the highest spot on the floor along these walls, and make all vertical measurements from this point. The standard height to the top of a wall cabinet is 84 inches, or 3 or 4 inches lower if the reach is too high for you. Using the level, mark a straight line along the walls at the height you choose. Next, measure the height of your cabinets and mark parallel lines along the walls for the bottoms of the cabinets. Finally, mark lines for the tops of the floor cabinets, adjusted if necessary for a raised or lowered countertop *(page 49).*

The width of a set of cabinets, of course, will depend upon your particular installation, but remember that ready-made cabinets will rarely fit the exact width of a wall. To fill the gaps, filler strips are available in 3- or 6-inch width, in the same material as the cabinets themselves. Trim the strips if necessary, and place them between cabinets of the same height—never at the end of a set.

Walls and floors are not flat—though cabinets are made as if they were—and you will have to shim outward or upward to make them level. If there are conspicuous gaps between the bottom of the cabinets and the wall, hide them with a wood shoe molding stained or painted to match the cabinets and nailed to the studs. To cover gaps between a kick space and the floor, use a vinyl cove molding *(page 20)*—a wood molding is likely to warp from spills and cleaning.

Readying the Walls

1 **Flattening a wall.** Using a carpenter's square or level, check the flatness of the walls within the lines you have marked for wall and floor cabinets. Wearing goggles, a respirator mask and a hat, sand down the high spots and bulges with a sanding block and garnet paper. For very high spots use a wood chisel and a power sander, checking constantly for flatness as you work.

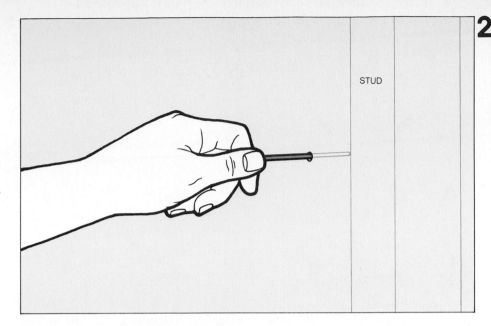

STUD

2 **Marking the studs.** Make a small pilot hole through the wall about 14 inches from the corner. Insert a length of stiff wire to locate the edge of the nearest stud, and measure ¾ inch beyond this point to the stud center. Use additional holes to determine whether the studs are set 16 or 24 inches apart. Finally, mark all the stud-center positions directly above the line for the top of floor cabinets and above and below the lines for wall cabinets.

The Right Way to Hang Cabinets

1 **Placing the first cabinet.** Remove the cabinet doors. Beginning at an inside corner, have a helper raise the first cabinet to the horizontal line marked for the tops of the cabinets. Check that the cabinet is level, then drill ⅛-inch pilot holes through the holding strips on the back of the cabinet and into the studs. Fasten the cabinet to the wall with 1½-inch, No. 6 screws, allowing some play for shimming (*bottom, right*). Check the fastened cabinet for horizontal level, and move the fastening screws if necessary.

2 **Shimming for plumb.** Check the edges of the cabinet for plumb and drive shims between the cabinet and wall wherever necessary, using narrow strips of smooth wood. If the cabinet is far out of plumb, loosen screws slightly to make room for the shims. When the cabinet is plumb, tighten the fastening screws and make a final check for both plumb and horizontal level. If you have forced the cabinet out of plumb, loosen the screws and reshim; if the cabinet is not level, remove it and reposition the screws.

3 **Fastening cabinets together.** Install subsequent cabinets along the wall, shimming them out to the same distance from the wall as the first one. As you hang each cabinet, secure it to the preceding one with a C clamp; protect the cabinet with pads of heavy cloth or strips of soft wood between the metal clamps and cabinets. For a cabinet up to 24 inches high, drill two ⅛-inch pilot holes, one third and two thirds of the distance from top to bottom, through the side of the front frame and into the preceding cabinet; drive 2½-inch, No. 6 screws into the holes and pull the cabinets snugly together. For higher cabinets use three screws, positioned at the top, bottom and middle of the frames.

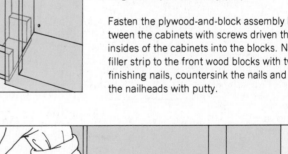

4 **Inserting a filler strip.** Set a filler strip between two installed cabinets and measure the distance from the back of the strip to the wall. Cut two pieces of ½-inch plywood to the width of the strip and the length of the distance you have measured; when fitted together at a right angle, the strip and the length of plywood should exactly match the depth of your cabinets. Carefully nail 1-by-3 (or, for a 6-inch strip, 1-by-6) blocks of wood to the ends of the plywood with twopenny finishing nails to make a long, U-shaped assembly (*left*).

Fasten the plywood-and-block assembly between the cabinets with screws driven through the insides of the cabinets into the blocks. Nail the filler strip to the front wood blocks with twopenny finishing nails, countersink the nails and cover the nailheads with putty.

Installing Floor Cabinets

Leveling with shims. Floor cabinets must be shimmed at both the wall and the floor to make them level and plumb. Slide the first cabinet into place at an inside corner, shimming it at the floor until it is level and meets the height of the line on the wall. Drive these shims in with a block of scrap wood to avoid dents and scratches in the floor or cabinet. Screw the cabinet to the wall (*page 47, Step 1*), checking to be sure that pulling the cabinet toward the wall does not tilt the top. Shim along the wall to make the cabinet plumb, then tighten the screws, checking again for level and plumb. Install additional cabinets and filler strips by the methods shown in Steps 3 and 4.

Setting Counters for Your Height

The standard countertop, which rises 36 inches from the floor can make an awkward working surface for someone considerably taller or shorter than the average human height. Raising or lowering the top is surprisingly simple and easy.

Of the two jobs, raising a countertop is somewhat more common. Before you begin, make a sort of dry run: Set strips of wood and a scrap sheet of plywood on the existing countertop, building it up to a comfortable working height. Then raise the real top to this height by either of two methods. The simpler method (below, right) is to remove the countertop and inset a strip of wood beneath it; the overhang of the top will hide the added strip somewhat, but the wood should match the cabinet and be prestained. By another method (above, right), which calls for raising the kick-space area, you can make a larger and less noticeable addition, but you must remove and replace the cabinet.

Counters can be lowered by as much as 2 inches, but no more—at least half the 4-inch kick plate must remain in place. For the dry run, use wood strips and plywood to raise a surface lower than the counter—a tabletop will do—to the height you want, then measure the difference between this height and the counter. To lower the counter, remove the cabinet from the wall and mark off the width of the strip that must be taken from the bottom of the kick plate. Draw straight lines completely around the plate with a carpenter's square to connect the marks, and cut along the lines with a saber or circular saw. Replace the cabinet with a fresh set of shims (page 48).

Raising the kick plate. Remove the cabinet from the wall and take off any molding that may cover the kick plate. Cut two strips of wood to raise the cabinet to the height you want, and to fit precisely across the front and back of the cabinet; cut two additional strips of the same thickness for the sides to fit snugly between the front and back strips. Fasten the wood strips to the bottom of the kick plate with wood screws driven through the strips and into the plate. Replace the cabinet with new shims (opposite, bottom). To re-cover the kick plate, apply a wide strip of vinyl cove molding (page 20), cut to fit if necessary.

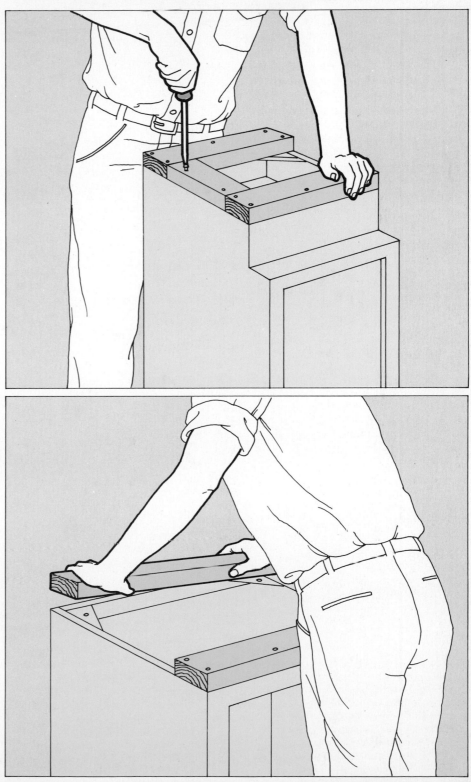

Raising the countertop. Remove the cabinet doors and unscrew the countertop from the diagonal braces in the top of the cabinet frame. Cut strips of wood to fit the top of the cabinet and screw them into place. Stain the face of the front wood strips to match the cabinet and replace the countertop with new screws long enough to bridge the new gap above the braces.

Reorganizing a Cabinet

Making full use of kitchen and bathroom cabinet space without sacrificing convenience is a challenge. Items get lost in high, inaccessible reaches, and extracting a pot or a soap bar nested in a low, deep cabinet requires deep knee bends. However, specialized hardware and spacesaving devices make it simple and economical to convert cabinets into convenient space misers. Many aids can be installed in existing cabinets to give the convenience of custom-made built-ins.

The first step in custom-fitting a cabinet to your needs is clearing the space in which to work. Once the permanently mounted shelving is removed *(Steps 1 and 2)*, the cabinet can be fitted with adjustable shelves; supports come ready to install and merely need to be screwed into place. For storage of large trays, vertical dividers *(opposite, bottom)* can be cut to size and slid into fixed tracks.

A variety of other spacesaving accessories can be fashioned with the aid of ready-made glides. Using them as supports for drawers or slide-out shelves *(opposite, top left)* eliminates the need to reach way back into dark cabinet interiors; kitchen and bathroom trash containers can be kept hidden yet accessible *(opposite, center);* even a sliding rack for hanging pots can be installed.

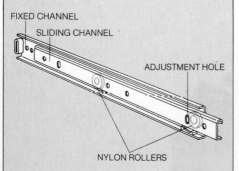

FIXED CHANNEL
SLIDING CHANNEL
ADJUSTMENT HOLE
NYLON ROLLERS

A versatile piece of hardware. Glides, which have two main components: a fixed channel that is screwed to a cabinet wall and a sliding channel that supports a drawer, can be used to mount a movable shelf, drawer or other slide-out convenience *(opposite)*. Nested between the two channels are ball bearings and nylon rollers. Oval screw holes allow for adjustment of the channel positions before mounting screws are tightened.

Removing Old Shelves

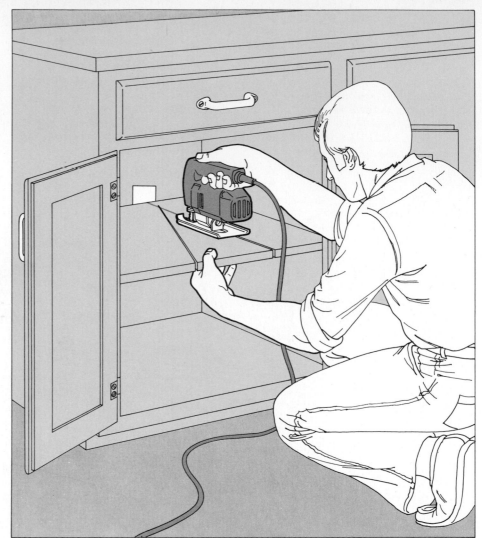

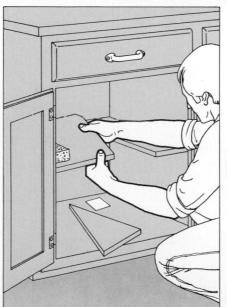

1 The first cut. Shelves are easy to remove if you saw a V that converges at the rear, making short, relief cuts—partially backing the saw in and out of the groove every few inches—to reduce binding of the tool as the shelf pieces sag. Use a keyhole saw to finish the rear cuts. A thin piece of tin or wood slipped between the shelf and rear wall will protect the finish from the saw blade.

2 Taking out the pieces. Tap the top and bottom of the shelf halves with a hammer several times to break the glue bond that holds the shelf in the dado joint. Then gently work the shelf up and down until it eases out of the dado. If the cabinet was built after 1950, when water-soluble polyvinyl glues began to replace insoluble animal glues, a wet sponge placed along the dado may help to loosen the bond. Once both shelf parts have been removed, fill the dado with wood putty (shrinkage during drying may necessitate a second application).

Glide-out Conveniences

Utility drawers. Drawer frames must have sides at least 1½ inches high for mounting the gliding hardware. Use rabbet *(inset)* or dado joints to withstand the stress of repeated pulling and pushing. Bottoms for most drawers can be made from thin plywood or hardboard, but if they must support heavy loads, they should be made of ½-inch plywood or tempered hardboard.

Pull-out pot rack. Mount a 1-by-2 on edge to span the top of the cabinet front to back as you would mount the track for a divider, suspending it as shown at bottom right if the door opening is framed. Attach the fixed channel from a set of glides to the side of this 1-by-2, and similarly mount the sliding channel on another 1-by-2. When the channels are engaged, the second board will slide in and out of the cabinet. Pothooks can be screwed into the bottom of the slider, or a perforated panel can be fastened to its side.

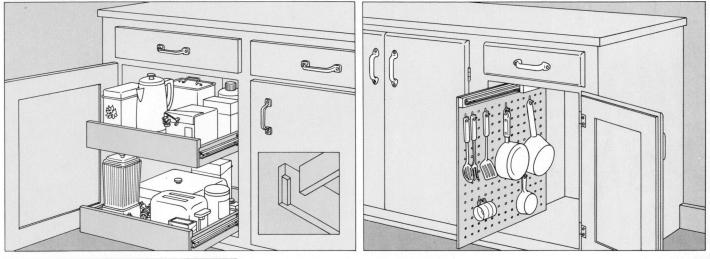

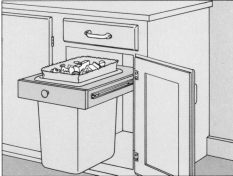

A disappearing container. Build a strong drawer *(above)* and mount it upside down on glides near the top of a cabinet. Near the middle of what would ordinarily be the bottom, saw a hole shaped and sized to support a lipped waste container at the desired level.

Partitions for Hard-to-store Utensils

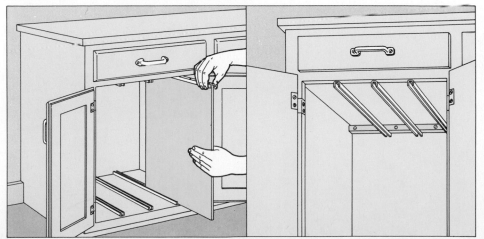

Adding vertical dividers. Screw onto the bottom of the cabinet metal, plastic or wood tracks—any strip with a U cross section will serve—as long as the cabinet is deep. If the door opening extends to the underside of the cabinet top *(far left)*, cut ⅜-inch plywood as wide as the cabinet is deep and ¼ inch shorter than the door opening. Slide the panels with top tracks into the bottom tracks, use a level to be sure they are vertical and draw lines to position the upper tracks. Screw the top tracks along these lines.

If the door opening has a frame *(left)*, the top tracks should be suspended so the dividers can slide out. Hang the top tracks between the bottom edge of the fascia in front and a crosswise level board screwed to the rear wall.

Wiring Designed to Meet Special Requirements

The variety of large and small appliances in a kitchen, and the combination of electricity and water-soaked surfaces in a bathroom are two circumstances that create electrical problems—the problem of overloaded circuits in the kitchen, of shock in the bathroom. The problems can be solved by improving existing wiring or installing new circuits.

The National Electrical Code recommends two separate 20-ampere circuits for small kitchen appliances; use the chart of average appliance wattages below to see whether you need more than two. A large appliance such as a dishwasher or a garbage disposal must have its own 20-ampere circuit; an electric range calls for a 50-ampere circuit. For all these appliances, large and small, you must tap a source of power and run electric cable to a convenient location.

Power for a single small use—a kitchen range fan or a light fixture over a work area—can usually be tapped from an existing ceiling box or receptacle box. Running new circuits is more complicated. Part of the job—connecting the circuit at the service panel—should be done by a professional electrician. But you can run cables for new circuits yourself and you can use a professional's method to run two cables at a time.

A kitchen circuit may call for a three-conductor cable, designed for 240-volt circuits and containing two 120-volt wires, color-coded black and red, and a white neutral wire. An electric range (page 55) or a wall-mounted oven, for instance, needs such a cable for the combination 120/240-volt circuit of its heating elements, lights, receptacles and timer. But a three-conductor cable can also reduce the number of separate cables running to the kitchen, saving the cost of extra cables. The circuits for a dishwasher and garbage disposal can be combined in a single three-conductor cable running to a junction box in the kitchen; from there, the circuits are split (page 55) and routed separately to the appliances. Two circuits for small appliances can run in a three-conductor cable to receptacles installed in the walls around counters and work areas, with the upper outlet of each receptacle on one circuit and the lower on another (page 54).

To get additional receptacles without having to cut into a wall for each one, use multioutlet assemblies—surface-mounted metal channels containing several prewired receptacles. The assemblies come in 3- to 6-foot lengths, with receptacles spaced 6, 12 or 18 inches apart; install four-outlet assemblies on separate circuits (page 54), or power a two-circuit assembly with a three-conductor cable.

Ensuring safety in the bathroom calls not for a special circuit, but a special protective device. The National Electrical Code requires this device, a ground-fault interrupter (GFI), in all new bathroom circuits, and adding a GFI to an existing circuit makes good sense in any bathroom. The GFI monitors a circuit for ground faults—current leaks caused by faulty wiring or damaged insulation. These leaks are too small to trip a circuit breaker, but they can be fatal to a bather standing on a wet floor. Within $\frac{1}{40}$ of a second of detecting such a ground fault, a GFI cuts off all power to the circuit.

GFIs are of two types: circuit breakers that should be installed in the service panel by an electrician, and special receptacles that can be installed by homeowners in a bathroom outlet box (page 55). If your bathroom has several receptacles, install the GFI at the first outlet on the circuit; in this location, it will protect all the receptacles beyond it.

Estimating circuit loads. Even a modest kitchen should have at least two separate 20-ampere circuits for small appliances, and you may need additional circuits if you are likely to run several high-wattage appliances simultaneously. Use the chart at right to estimate the maximum load on your kitchen circuits. The chart gives average wattages for a wide range of appliances. Combine wattages to determine a total simultaneous load; to convert watts to amperes, divide by the voltage (120). For example, if a coffee maker and a toaster-oven are in use at the same time, the total load on the circuit would be 2,100 watts, or 17.5 amperes. This is close to the maximum safe load for a 20-ampere circuit—place each of the appliances on a separate circuit, possibly by plugging them into a receptacle fed by a split 240-volt cable (page 54).

Appliance Power Ratings

Appliance	Wattage
Blender	300
Broiler	1,140
Coffee maker	600
Deep fryer	1,350
Food mixer	150
Frying pan	1,200
Refrigerator	250
Rotisserie	1,400
Sandwich grill	1,200
Toaster	1,100
Toaster-oven	1,500

Running Cable and Tapping Power

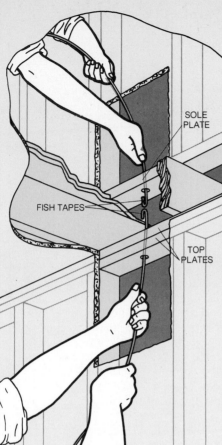

SOLE PLATE

FISH TAPES

TOP PLATES

Cables between floors. To bring power to an upstairs kitchen or bathroom, cut a hole approximately 16 by 16 inches between wall studs at ceiling height on the lower floor. Make a similar opening at floor level on the upper floor. Using an electric drill equipped with an extension bit *(below, right)*, drill holes for the cable through the exposed top and sole plates—¾-inch holes for a No. 12 cable, 1 inch for a pair of cables. With the aid of a helper, hook two fish tapes together *(left)* between the plates. Pull the upper tape down, attach the cable to it *(bottom, left)* and draw the cable up through the plates.

Cables inside walls. Cut holes for outlet boxes between studs, either 12 inches above the floor or, as shown below, 44 to 46 inches above the floor for countertop outlets. Expose the studs between openings with 4-by-2-inch access holes, cut at the same height as baseboard outlets or about 8 inches below countertop level (cabinets will hide the patches that close these holes). Using an extension bit, drill cable holes through the studs, as nearly parallel to the wall as possible. Working through the outlet and access holes, hook fish tapes together and pull the cable through the studs and to each outlet.

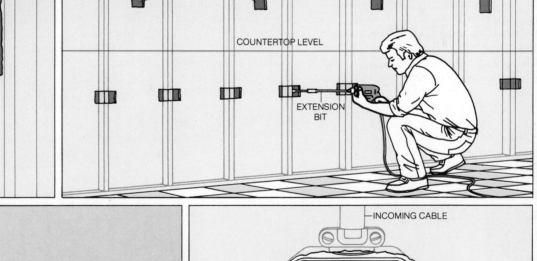

OUTLET-BOX HOLES

COUNTERTOP LEVEL

EXTENSION BIT

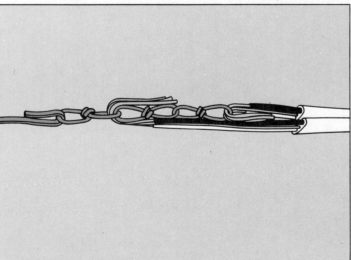

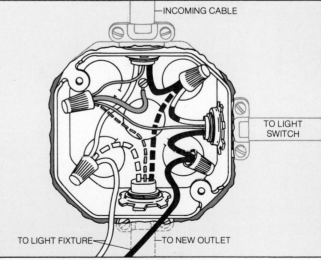

INCOMING CABLE

TO LIGHT SWITCH

TO LIGHT FIXTURE

TO NEW OUTLET

Running two cables at once. Strip about 2½ inches of insulation from the end of one cable, about 5 inches from the other, and 1½ inches from their wires. Hook one cable to the end link of a short, light chain and the other to a link about 1½ inches farther along; hook the end of a fish tape to the other end of the chain *(above)*. Wrap electrician's tape over each connection. Have a helper feed the cables to you, and pull the fish tape through studs or plates.

Tapping power from a ceiling box. Remove the light fixture from a ceiling box and examine the wiring. If you see only one cable, do not use the box as a power source: the power would be interrupted whenever the wall switch is turned off. If two or more cables enter the box *(above)*, connect the black wire of the new cable *(dashed lines)* to the black wire of the incoming cable, the white wire to the other neutral wires and the bare wire to the other ground wires.

Circuits for Heavy Demands

Two receptacle circuits in one cable. To install a number of double receptacles, with each pair served by different circuits, run a three-conductor, No. 12 cable from the service panel to an outlet box 3½ inches deep, and additional lengths of cable from one oversized outlet box to another. With a pair of needle-nose pliers, break the brass jumper strip connecting the two brass terminals on each receptacle *(inset)*.

At all but the last receptacle, fasten a short length of black-insulated wire to one of the brass terminals and to the two black cable wires; a red wire to the other brass terminal and to the two red cable wires; and a white wire to either of the two silver terminals and to the two white cable wires. Connect all bare cable wires to each other and to grounding screws on the box and receptacle *(right)*. At the end-of-the-run receptacle, connect the color-coded wires directly to the screw terminals.

A surface-mounted receptacle strip. Run a two-conductor, No. 12 cable from the service panel to a point about 8 inches above a countertop. Clamp the cable to a knockout in the base of a multioutlet assembly *(right)* and screw the base to the wall. Cut the black, white and green wires of the assembly at a point near the incoming power cable and strip ½ inch of insulation from each wire. Use pressure-type wire connectors *(inset)* to join the incoming black and white wires to the matching assembly wires *(right, below)*. Electrical codes do not allow the use of these connectors for ground wires; use a wire cap or a crimp-type connector to join the two green assembly wires, the bare cable wire and a short grounding jumper wire. Then fasten the other end of the jumper wire to the assembly base with a grounding screw.

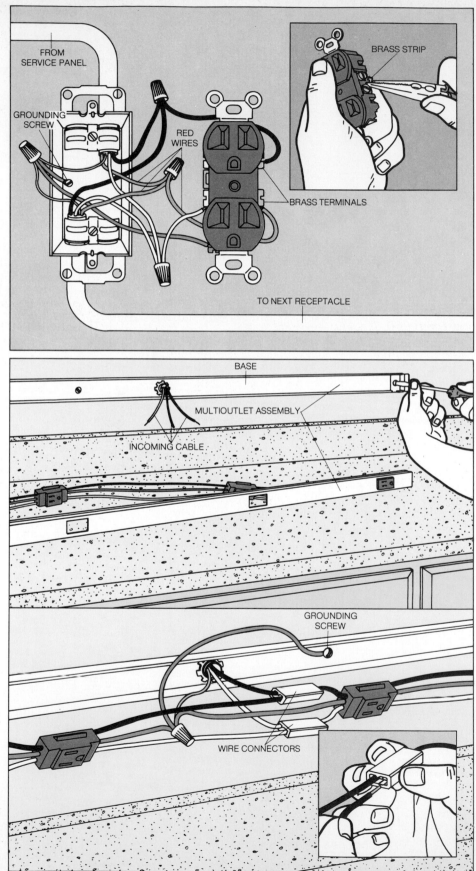

Two circuits at a kitchen sink. To provide separate circuits for a dishwasher and garbage disposal, run a single three-conductor cable, wired for 240 volts, from the service panel to a junction box in the kitchen. In the junction box *(right)*, connect the black wire from the service panel to the white wire of the switch cable; paint or tape both ends of the white wire black to mark it as a voltage-carrying conductor. Connect the black wire of the switch cable to the black wire of the disposal cable. Join the red wire of the service-panel cable to the black wire of the dishwasher cable. Fasten the three remaining white wires with a wire cap and connect all bare ground wires to each other and to the junction box. Complete the connections at the switch and appliances and screw a cover plate over the junction box.

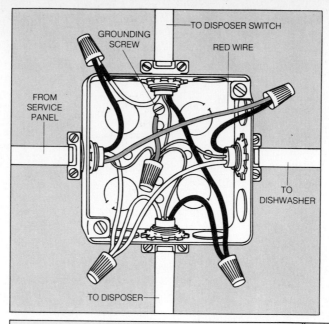

Wiring a 120/240-volt electric range. Run a three-conductor, No. 6 cable from the service panel through a hole in the floor to a 50-ampere receptacle mounted on the wall near the back of the range. Push the white cable wire into the receptacle terminal marked W and tighten the screw; attach the red and black wires to the two other terminals and fasten the bare ground wire to the back of the receptacle.

To connect the range to the receptacle, use a three-wire cord, called a pigtail, with a matching plug and connection lugs. At the terminal block on the back of the range, join the white pigtail wire to the center terminal and the black and red wires to the two other terminals. Ground the range frame according to local electrical codes, using either a built-in grounding strap *(right)* connected to the neutral terminal or a No. 10 grounding wire fastened to the frame and to a grounding clamp on a cold-water pipe.

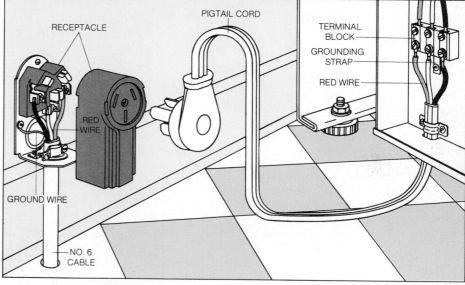

Shockproofing a Receptacle

Installing a ground-fault interrupter. Turn off power and remove the existing receptacle. If the outlet box is less than 2¾ inches deep, screw a spacer plate to the box to make more room for wiring. Attach the black and white GFI leads marked LINE to the corresponding wires of the incoming power cable, and the black and white leads marked LOAD to the corresponding wires in the cable going to the next receptacle; if the circuit has no other outlet, cap the LOAD leads with wire caps. Connect the green GFI wire to the cable ground wires and to a grounding jumper wire secured to the outlet box. Screw the GFI to the spacer and complete the installation with a cover plate.

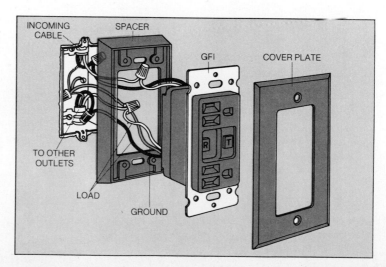

Clearing the Air of Odors, Smoke and Moisture

Kitchens and bathrooms require fan-powered ventilation ducted to the outside of the house to remove odors and greasy smoke as well as water vapor, which can condense into moisture that mists mirrors and windows and, more important, damages walls and floors. In a bathroom, a simple wall or ceiling exhaust fan will eliminate condensation. For a kitchen, the ducted blower fan in a canopy hood above the range is generally most effective, although a simple through-the-wall fan may be easier to install. Ductless blower fans also are made for range hoods but this type only filters grease and smoke, churning heat and moisture back into the kitchen.

Metal shells for range hoods are made in a variety of sizes to be mounted under cabinets or on walls or suspended from ceilings. The shells have knockout sections to which ducts and wiring are connected. Most range hoods come with a squirrel-cage-type blower fan and a light prewired to switches on the front of the hood. The wiring terminates in a junction box in the hood; it must be connected to a wall receptacle or junction box.

Wall and ceiling blowers for bathrooms are installed in much the same way as range hoods, though you may need to add a wall switch for the fan.

The duct connecting an exhaust fan to the outdoors should be as straight as possible. Its length and the number of elbows in it will affect your choice of blower fans since long runs resist the push of the fan and elbows add still more resistance—a 90° elbow creates as much resistance as 10 feet of duct.

An exit in an outside wall is preferable, with horizontal duct runs from the kitchen pitched slightly downward to keep grease from flowing back to the fan; but roof venting may be necessary. In some cases you may have to vent a downstairs bathroom or a kitchen "island" range through the roof, running duct up through one or more floors and concealing it in a closet or a wallboard enclosure. In cold climates, insulate any duct that passes through the attic to limit condensation. In an older house, you may be able to run duct into an unused flue.

Fans are rated in cubic feet of air moved per minute (CFM). A fan venting directly through an outside wall should have a CFM rating equal to the number of cubic feet in the room divided by 4 for a kitchen or by 7.5 for a bathroom. For a range hood set against an inside wall, use a fan rated at 40 times the number of feet

of duct you will use. For fans set over ranges in island or peninsula counters, multiply duct length by 50. Add 50 to 100 CFM for duct runs longer than 10 feet. Variable-speed fans are usually more satisfactory than single-speed ones.

For most kitchen installations, round steel duct 7 inches in diameter is easiest to install, though you may need rectangular duct if you plan to conceal it between studs inside a wall. For bathroom installation, 3-inch or 4-inch duct is generally specified; in this size, flexible plastic duct is easier to handle and to bend around corners than steel. Wrap all duct connections with duct tape.

Where the duct run ends on the outside wall of the house or on the roof, install a wall or roof cap. A wall cap usually comes with a hinged damper to close the duct passageway to back drafts and a screen to keep out birds and insects.

Clean the grease filter of a kitchen vent hood once a week with hot, soapy water. Every six months shut off the power and remove and clean the blower; at the same time, clean the hood interior and as much of the duct as you can reach conveniently. Removing a large build-up of grease deep in the ductwork may be a job for a professional.

Installing a Hood for a Kitchen Fan

1 **Making the duct opening.** Remove the knockouts in the range hood for attaching the duct and the wiring. Hold the hood in place while a helper reaches underneath to mark the outline of the duct opening on the kitchen wall or cabinet bottom *(left)*. Disconnect at the main service panel all electrical circuits going to or through the kitchen. With a keyhole saw, cut around the outline, staying ¼ inch outside the mark. If the fan is to exhaust directly out of the wall behind the range, cut a hole for the duct in the outside wall. If the opening must go through a stud, remove a segment of stud and frame around the opening as on page 61.

2 **Making the duct connection.** Attach a hood collar, provided by the manufacturer, to the round or rectangular duct opening in the hood. Use sheet-metal screws driven through preformed holes in the collar and the hood. Depending on the direction in which the duct will run, attach a length of duct or an elbow to the collar.

3 **Mounting the hood.** Drill ⅛-inch holes through the cabinet bottom at the locations of the mounting slots, spacing out a recessed cabinet bottom with wood strips (below) as necessary. If there is no cabinet from which to hang the hood, support it with right-angle brackets. A hood over a range in an island or a peninsula away from a wall can be attached to ceiling joists or to a soffit built down from the ceiling.

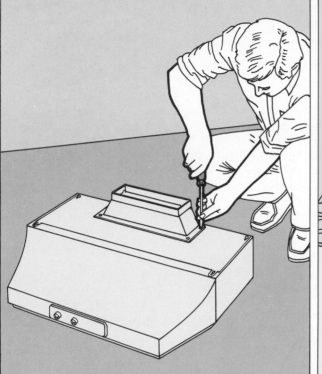

Three Routes for Ducting

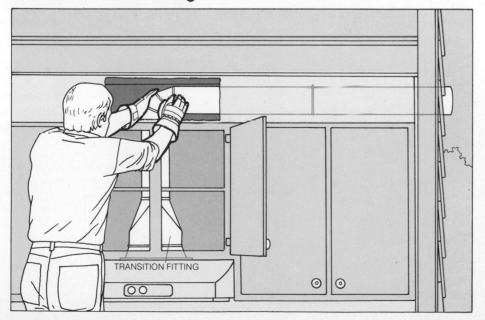

TRANSITION FITTING

Using a soffit. If the vent opening is in the cabinet bottom, and if—as is likely—there is open or enclosed space between the tops of the cabinets and the ceiling, run duct up to the soffit and attach an elbow. To connect round duct to a rectangular vent collar, use the transition fitting shown at left. Cut a hole slightly more than 7 inches in diameter through the outside wall. From outside, insert 7-inch round steel duct and connect it to the elbow. You can hide the duct, if necessary, by framing the space above the cabinets and covering it with wallboard.

If there is no space above the cabinets, you can run ducts in the same way through holes cut in the sides of adjoining cabinets.

Dodging a brick wall. In a single-story brick house you can avoid the chore of cutting through masonry by running duct up into attic space and down through an eave—circling around the top course of the brick wall. Just within the wall install a transition fitting to adapt round to rectangular duct.

Going through the roof. If the most convenient route for the duct is through the roof, run duct straight up, through a hole in the ceiling between two joists, through a corresponding hole in the attic floor and out through a hole in the roof between two rafters. You may have to angle the duct slightly to avoid joists and rafters.

Covering the Outside End

Attaching a wall cap. Cut off ducting that protrudes beyond the house siding. Fit a flanged wall cap over the end of the duct; be sure that the cap fits tightly around the duct and that the hinged damper swings freely. Caulk under the flange to make a weathertight seal.

Installing a roof cap. Trim away protruding duct ½ inch above the roof surface, cutting at the same angle as the roof pitch. Pull out the trimmed section of ducting. The top edge of the flashing attached to the roof cap should be slipped under the shingles around the hole in the roof.

Cut away shingles that keep the roof cap from fitting over the hole. Working from below, reinstall the duct section. Coat the underside of the roof-cap flashing with roofing cement and press it into place. Apply roofing cement to the underside of shingles that overlap the flashing.

Hooking Up the Fan

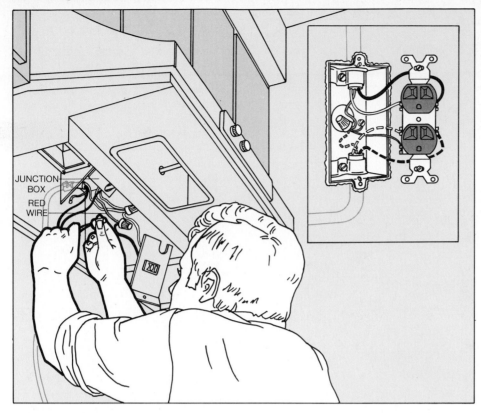

JUNCTION
BOX
RED
WIRE

Wiring a range hood. Turn off current to the room. Run cable to a nearby wall receptacle or junction box as shown on page 53. Attach the black and white wires of the cable (*inset, dash lines*) to the unused terminals on the receptacle. Connect the ground wire from the cable to the ground wire of the receptacle and use a jumper wire to connect the pair to the grounding screw in the outlet box. At the hood, attach the other end of the cable to the wires at a junction box according to the manufacturer's instructions, and screw the cover of the box in place.

In the typical model shown here, connections are made between the white hood, cable and motor-receptacle wires, between the black hood and cable wires, and between the black motor-receptacle wire and the red hood wire. Screw the ground wire of the cable to the hood. Finally, follow the instructions for your model to mount the blower unit and install the light bulb, light lens and grease filter.

Installing a Fan in a Bathroom Ceiling

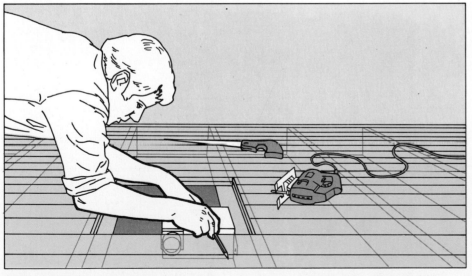

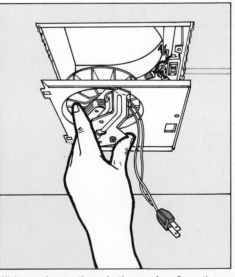

Making the holes. Locate a ceiling joist by probing. Select a location for the fan between joists. For a location below an attic, drill a locator hole through the ceiling and on through the attic floor above. Remove enough attic flooring to accommodate the fan housing. Detach the housing and set it alongside the joist and over the locator hole. Cut a hole in the ceiling to fit the housing. Screw the housing to the joist, its lip flush with the ceiling. For a location below an-

other room, remove enough ceiling material to enable you to mount the housing from below.

If you plan to vent the fan through an outside wall, cut a duct hole in the wall. If you must vent the fan through the roof, cut a hole in the roof as shown above. From a downstairs bathroom, cut a hole for the duct at a convenient place in the floor of the room above and corresponding holes in the ceiling of that room and the attic floor above.

Wiring and mounting a bathroom fan. Open the outlet box cover in the fan housing. Run cable through a connector installed in the outlet box and attach the cable to the coded terminals in the box. Mount the motor-fan assembly in the housing. Turn off the current to the bathroom. Run cable from the fan to a light switch and attach it in the same way as for the kitchen fan or, if you want the fan to operate independently of the bathroom light, wire it to a separate switch.

Spacesavers: Recessed Cabinets and Appliances

A spacesaving way of installing a cabinet, a heater or an intercom in a handy location is to recess it into a wall, like a medicine chest. Almost any wall in your house will serve but how you install it depends on the nature of the wall.

Your wall will probably be built of 2-by-4 studs spaced 16 or 24 inches on center. Since a nominal 2-by-4 is actually 1½ by 3½ inches, the space between adjoining studs will be 14½ or 22½ inches. Most vanity cabinets and other types of appliances are designed to fit either a 14½-inch opening or the 30½-inch opening that results from the removal of a single stud, although units of intermediate dimensions are also available.

A recessed unit sits on a sill inside the recess and is attached to studs or supplementary braces at the sides of the aperture. It usually has a door or a cover plate that covers the edges of the opening. If you want to install a wall recess for a toaster or a telephone, however, you simply open a nook in a wall, attach a shelf of 1-inch lumber to the sill and then patch with wallboard around the edges of the opening.

Installations are easiest when the location is not critical; then the position of the existing studs can dictate the exact location and little or no additional framing is needed. But if the unit must be centered on a wall or above a lavatory, you generally have to remove any intervening studs and construct supplementary framing—both to replace the removed studs and to provide nailing surfaces for patching the wall.

The amount of extra framing will depend on whether you are working in a nonbearing wall—one running parallel to the joists—or a bearing wall, which is perpendicular to the joists. If the joists in your house are concealed by ceilings and floors, you can usually figure out which way the joists run by studying floor and ceiling nailing patterns. If you must work on a bearing wall, the support lost by removal of studs must be replaced, and you may need to provide temporary support (page 62) during the work.

All exterior walls must be treated as bearing walls, and present special problems in addition. Most are filled with insulation and contain crosspieces that act as fire stops. Since outside walls are cold, moisture vapor in the interior atmosphere tends to condense on and rust steel equipment mounted in them.

Before cutting an opening in a wall, trace the wiring and plumbing pipes and try to avoid them; plumbing, especially, is tedious to reroute. An electrical outlet nearby, however, is necessary for a lighted cabinet or an appliance. Before cutting into any wall that is likely to contain wiring, make sure to turn off the power to that circuit.

Making Recesses in Nonbearing Walls

Recessing between two studs. If the recess can be an exact fit between two studs, probe with a wire to find the stud at either side of the proposed location (page 47, top). Alongside the stud, draw on the wall the dimensions of the opening desired, using a level to get the top and bottom lines horizontal. Cut out that section of wall surface. Drive a sixpenny nail into each stud 1½ inches above the top edge of the opening. Use these nails to position a 2-by-4 cut to fit the opening and toenail it into the studs to form a header. Similarly toenail a 2-by-4 just below the opening to form a sill.

Cutting Intervening Studs

1 **Removing intervening studs.** If the recess must be wider than the space between studs, locate the two studs on either side of the proposed opening. Between them mark on the wall horizontal lines 1½ inches above and 1½ inches below the proposed location of the cabinet. Cut out the wall surface bounded by these lines and the two side studs. With a backsaw, sever the intervening studs even with the top and the bottom of the opening. Carefully pry the severed segments away from the wall. Some of the heads of the nails holding the wallboard to the stud on the other side of the wall probably will pull through the wallboard, and you will have to repair a few small damaged areas in that wall.

2 **Framing the opening.** Install a header and a sill of 2-by-4 segments nailed to the severed ends of the intervening studs; use a pair of eightpenny nails for each stud. For added strength, toenail the header and sill to the side studs.

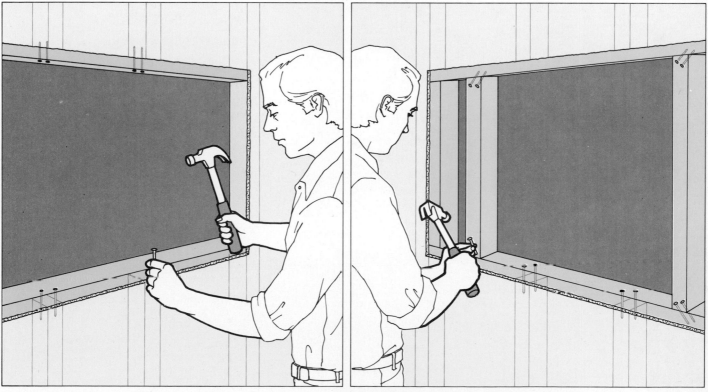

3 **Narrowing the opening.** If the recess is to be narrower than the opening thus created, nail 2-by-4 vertical pieces to the studs to provide a nailing surface for wallboard. Cut two 2-by-4s the height of the recess and toenail them to the sill and header on each side of the desired recess. Fill the spaces around the recess with wallboard patches nailed to the vertical 2-by-4s.

Making Recesses inside a Bearing Wall

1 Preparing the opening. On a bearing wall determine the size and position of the opening you need and draw its outline on the wall between two studs, allowing 5½ inches extra at top and bottom to accommodate a header and a sill. Remove the section of wall surface. Cut and pry out the stud as described on page 61. If you must saw through two or more studs, brace the ceiling on both sides of the wall before cutting.

For a ceiling brace, use a 2-by-4 longer than the aperture is wide. Support it about 30 inches out from the wall by jamming between it and the floor as many vertical 2-by-4s as the number of studs you will cut. If the 2-by-4 props are a bit short, shim underneath them to keep the bracing snug. Saw out segments of intervening studs. If the saw binds, tighten the shims.

2 Installing the frame. Make a header of two 2-by-6s, set side by side on edge at the top of the opening. Toenail each 2-by-6 to the side studs and to the ends of the severed studs. Install a similar sill. Cut segments of 2-by-4 the length of the distance between the header and the sill and nail them to the side studs. If necessary, toenail additional vertical 2-by-4s between the header and sill as shown on page 61. Remove the ceiling supports.

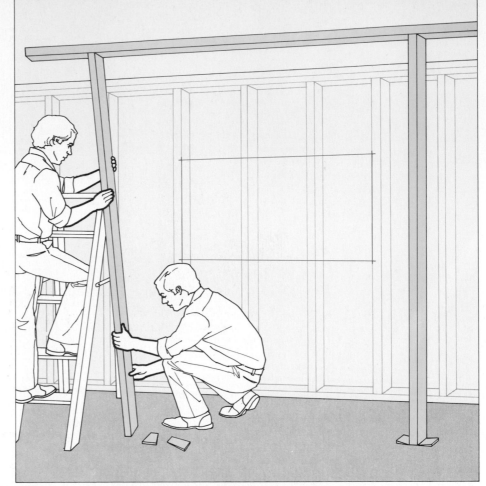

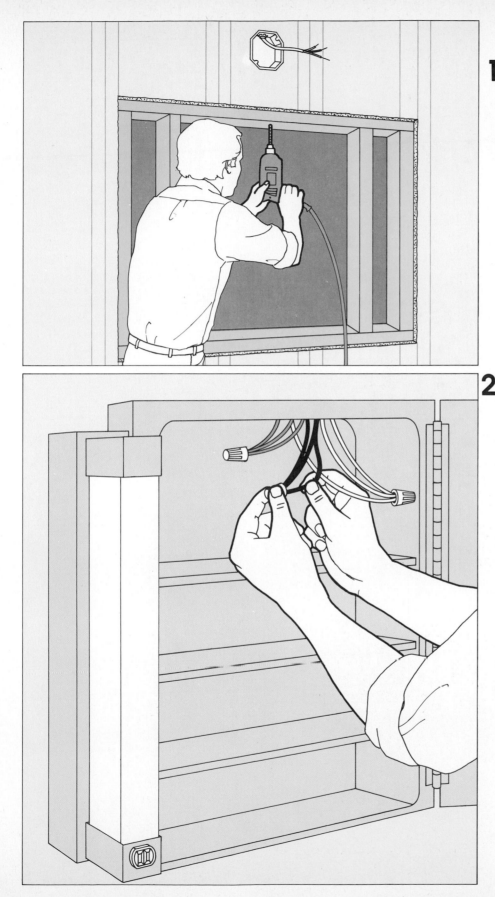

Wiring for Cabinet Lights

1 **Preparing the wiring.** Bring a cable to the recess from a convenient outlet box (*pages 52-54*) after turning off power to that circuit. If the wall opening is framed with one 2-by-4 header, drill a ½-inch hole through it that will mate with the wiring access hole in the top of the cabinet. Lead the cable through the hole in the header.

If the opening is framed by a header made of two 2-by-6s on edge there will be room to lead the cable behind the header and into the opening.

2 **Making the connections.** Rest the bottom edge of the cabinet on the sill and lead the cable end through the opening in the top of the cabinet and into the wiring compartment. Anchor the cable with the cable clamp on top of the cabinet. Secure the cabinet to studs or braces inside the aperture. With a wire cap, connect the ground wire of the cable to a green wire from the cabinet or, if there is no green wire, connect the ground wire to a green grounding screw. Connect the white wires from the cable and from the cabinet with a wire cap. Similarly connect the black cable wire to the black (or sometimes red) cabinet wire. Restore the power.

Making a Sauna from a Box, a Bench and a Heater

A sauna, an insulated wood box that provides a dry-heat bath, can be tucked into a corner of a bathroom, basement or garage—or expanded to fill most of a spare bedroom. The top is always low—6½ to 7 feet is ideal for keeping the heat where it belongs—so a sauna can fit under any normal ceiling. The floor space for a one-person unit can be as little as 9 square feet; each additional bather requires only about 7 more square feet. A family-sized unit in Finland, where saunas were invented, usually covers about 36 square feet and holds a two-tiered bench with both seats large enough for lying on: 20 inches wide and 6 feet long.

A modern unit operates with an electric heater. Because the paneling is unfinished wood, it remains comfortable to touch even when the heater brings the bath to the ideal 190°.

Building the sauna calls only for simple woodworking and wiring. The walls can be framed and the ceiling fabricated on the floor, then raised into place (right). The bench frame, however, must be assembled in place because it is permanently anchored to the wall opposite the heater (page 67). The bench seat is made separately and is removable for cleaning. The tongue-and-groove paneling and the bench can be redwood, cedar or white pine, but it must be seasoned lumber; pitch pockets and sappy knots in green lumber get hot. For the same reason, all of the nailheads must be set and the screws countersunk so that they cannot be touched accidentally.

Room walls can provide outer covering for one or two sauna walls, but the outside of the others are sheathed with wallboard. The floor under the box may be left bare if it is concrete, or covered with a simple wood grid.

Most materials you will need are available at lumberyards, but the heater and special sauna door must be ordered from a sauna dealer. The manufacturer will supply instructions for connecting the heater you buy. Small ones usually can run off the power from the nearest 120-volt junction box; larger ones require a 240-volt line connected to the service panel. You may want to leave the panel connections to a professional, but running the power cable from the panel to the sauna is the same as for 120 volts. The door, which is solid wood with a double-strength window to admit light, comes prehung (page 68). By buying both the heater and door in advance, you can plan their locations and requisite framing when you plot dimensions for the sauna.

Constructing the Box

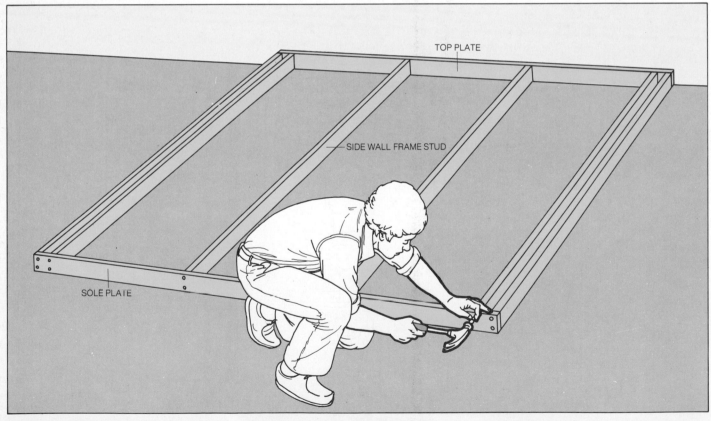

1 Framing the walls. Working on the floor, assemble each frame of 2-by-4s. The top and sole plates for the front and back wall frames are cut to the inside width of the sauna; plates for the side walls are 7 inches longer than the inside depth. Cut studs 3 inches shorter than the ceiling height, and set them between the ends of the plates and at intervals of about 24 inches. For the door, leave a space ½ inch wider than the jamb. Secure the plates to the studs with tenpenny nails. For each side frame, add an extra stud 2 inches inside each end stud. For the door header, nail a 2-by-4 crosswise between the studs ¼ inch farther from the floor than the finished height of the top of the doorjamb.

2 **Erecting the wall frames.** After removing the baseboard (*page 8*), set the back frame flat against the room wall, leaving a 3½-inch space at the end for a side frame if you plan to locate the sauna in a corner. Using a carpenter's level, plumb the back frame and add shims as needed to make it absolutely vertical. Toenail the top plate into each stud of the room wall, or secure the plate with masonry nails 18 inches apart if the wall is concrete.

If the floor is wood, secure the sole plate with tenpenny nails 18 inches apart. If the floor is concrete, use a ½-inch masonry bit to drill through the plate into the floor at 18-inch intervals, tap in ¼-inch lead anchors and secure the plate with washers and 2½-inch screws. Nail the side wall frames to the back frame at the corners. Set the front frame between the sides and nail. Anchor these frames to the floor, then saw out the sole plate between the doorframe studs.

3 **Fabricating the ceiling.** The ceiling is a 2-by-4 frame sheathed in plywood, filled with insulation and paneled inside with tongue-and-groove boards (*below*). Make front and back plates as long as the outside width of the sauna, joists 3 inches shorter than the sauna; nail joists between plates every 24 inches. Nail ¼-inch plywood to the joists at 12-inch intervals. Flip the ceiling over. Staple 3½-inch fiberglass batts between joists, vapor barrier toward you. Nail boards over the insulation, at right angles to the joists, setting the groove side of the first flush with the frame edge and drive four eightpenny nails along the frame edge. Then drive and countersink nails at a 45° angle into each joist through the corner at the base of the tongue (*inset*). Nail successive boards only along the tongue side. Cut the tongue edge off the last board within ½ inch of the edge of the frame; nail the board to the frame edge.

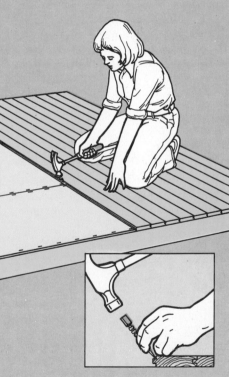

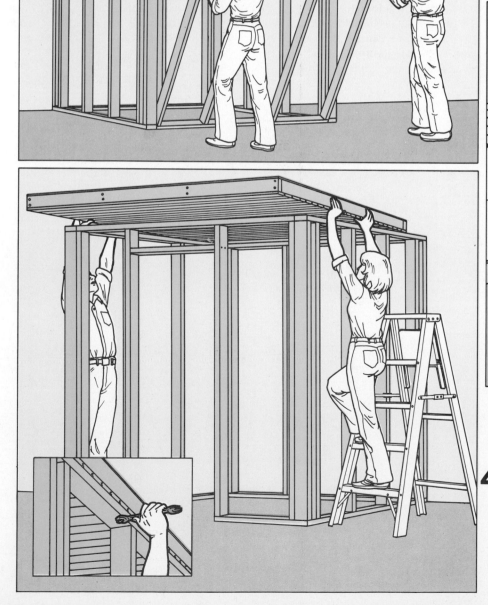

4 **Installing the ceiling.** After drilling two ¼-inch holes in the top plate of each wall frame, ¾ inch from the outer edge and a third of the way from each corner, set the ceiling on top of the wall frames, paneled side down. Align the edges. Then drill 3⁄16-inch pilot holes into the ceiling through the ¼-inch holes in the wall frame. Insert washers and ¼-inch lag screws 3 inches long, using a wrench to tighten them securely (*inset*).

Finishing the Walls

1 Bringing in power. Run No. 8 gauge copper cable rated for temperatures to 194° from the nearest junction box *(pages 52-55)*—or from the service panel if 240 volts are required—to the heater, which is usually placed against the front wall or on a side wall near the front. If you lead the cable in from a room wall, drill a ¾-inch hole through each stud of the side and front frame to the heater location. For a heater with built-in controls and relays, drill the holes 1 foot above the sole plate or at the heater mounting height specified by the manufacturer. For a heater with separate controls, drill the holes at a convenient height for mounting the control and relay box outside the sauna.

If you lead the cable in from the room ceiling, drill a ¾-inch hole just inside the top edge of the sauna ceiling and through the top plate of the wall frame next to the stud that lies nearest to the location of the heater.

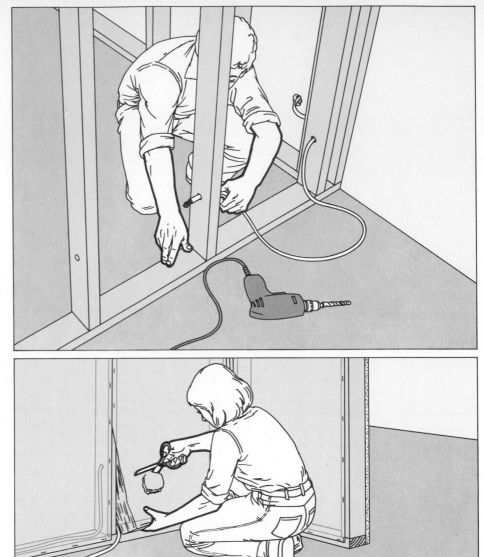

2 Venting and insulating. The sauna walls are filled with fiberglass batts—foil vapor barrier to the outside—then vented and sheathed with wallboard. If your sauna door does not have a vent, cut a 3-inch hole about 6 inches above the floor in the wall behind or next to the heater and snip a matching hole through the insulation. Cut another vent hole 3 inches square at the back opposite the heater and about 8 inches below the ceiling. Working outside the sauna, cover each vent hole with a metal vent plate.

3 Paneling the walls. Measure the height of the back wall, deduct the width of one tongue of your paneling and then divide the total by the width of a paneling strip. If the last strip will be less than half a board, increase its width to half and use a circular or table saw to rip the amount of the increase from the groove side of the first strip. Panel from the bottom up. Rip the back edge of the tongue side of the top strip to a 45° angle *(inset)*; place the groove of the top strip over the tongue of the preceding strip and tap the board to swing it back against the studs. Nail the top strip straight into the top plate of the wall near the ceiling. Set the nailheads. Panel the front wall and then the side walls similarly, cutting the strips before securing them to leave the vent hole exposed. If your heater has built-in controls, drill a ¾-inch hole and feed the cable through the strip at the heater mounting location before securing the strip. Cover each vent hole with a wood vent plate.

Building a Single Bench

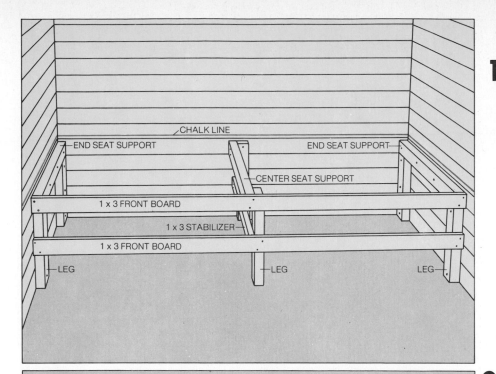

CHALK LINE

END SEAT SUPPORT

END SEAT SUPPORT

CENTER SEAT SUPPORT

1 x 3 FRONT BOARD

1 x 3 STABILIZER

1 x 3 FRONT BOARD

LEG

LEG

LEG

1 **Constructing the frame.** Using 2-by-3s, make seat end supports 1½ inches shorter than the bench and legs 3 inches shorter than the bench height. Nail the end supports and legs to the side walls. Provide additional support at 36-inch intervals—a 2-by-3 seat support, a 1-by-3 stabilizer 1½ inches shorter than bench width, and legs ½ inch shorter than bench height. Face-nail the legs to the ends of the support, turn the assembly over and nail the stabilizer to the legs 6 inches from the bottoms. Secure the legs of the center support to the back wall with finishing nails. To tie the frame together, cut two 1-by-3s the length of the bench and nail these boards to the front of the supports at the top and 6 inches above the floor.

2 **Assembling the seat.** Using 2-by-3s, cut a cleat— as long as the bench is deep—to fit between each pair of legs. To find how many 1-by-3 slats you need, divide the bench depth by three. Cut the slats ¼ inch shorter than the length of the bench. Lay the cleats in position on the floor and arrange the slats across them, broadside down. Let the front slat overlap the front of the cleats by 1¾ inches and leave ½ inch of cleat protruding behind the back slat; space the remaining slats evenly between the front and back. Round the top edges of the slats with sandpaper, then nail the slats to the cleats with sixpenny finishing nails. Set all nailheads. Place the seat on the bench frame, but do not fasten it; you can remove it easily for cleaning.

Adding a Second Tier

Connecting the tiers. Frame a simple bench (*Step 1, above*) 32 inches high. Then, in front of it, assemble end supports and legs for another simple bench 16 inches high. To support the front bench at each 36-inch interval, cut a 2-by-3 support and a 1-by-3 stabilizer 2½ inches longer than the seat depth. For each support, cut one leg 15½ inches long and nail it to the front end of the support. Nail the back end of the support to the front leg of the support on the back bench. Nail the stabilizer to the front leg of the front support and the front leg of the back bench. Attach front boards to the front frame. Then make two identical seats for the frames.

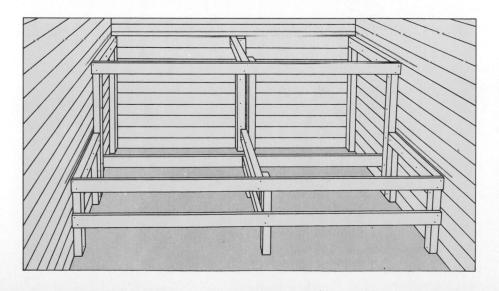

Installing a Door and Heater

Installing the prehung door. Position the door unit in its rough opening to open outward, wedging it in place with pieces of cardboard. Insert two evenly spaced wood shims between the top of the jamb and the header and three along each side of the jamb to maintain a ¼-inch clearance between the jamb and the outer stud frame. (On the hinge side of the jamb, the shims cannot be evenly spaced; set a shim just below each hinge and a third shim midway between them.) Drive a pair of tenpenny finishing nails through the jamb and each shim into the frame. Knock off the protruding ends of the shims and remove the cardboard strips to free the door. Nail the interior and exterior doorcasing around the jamb with sixpenny finishing nails.

Building a heater fence. A picket fence set at least 4 inches past the heater shields it. Cut a pair of 1-by-2 fence rails to reach from the wall 4 inches beyond the heater. Set the rails parallel on the floor, spaced as far apart as the height of the rocks in the heater. Cut seven 1-by-2 fence pickets and nail them across the rails, one at each end and the rest spaced evenly between. Build a similar but narrower panel, with fewer pickets, for the side of the heater. Nail a 2-by-2 post vertically to each wall just inside the point where the fence will attach. Nail each of the fence panels to a post and butt nail the free ends of the rails together at the corner.

Wiring the heater. Because heater wiring systems differ, check the manufacturer's instructions for your own unit. In the typical medium-capacity, 240-volt unit shown at right, the two red or black hot wires, white neutral wire and green or copper ground wire of the power cable are connected to like-colored wires in the relay box. The flexible cable from the relay box runs into the sauna where it is secured to the heater with a cable clamp; its black, red (*shown here as gray*), and green wires join wires of the same colors at the heater. The thermostat sensor passes into the sauna through a hole in the wall and is stapled behind a protective cover within 6 inches of the ceiling.

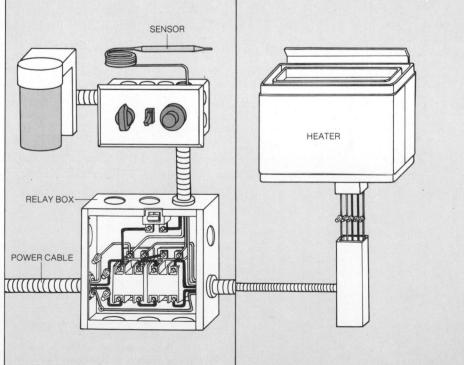

SENSOR

RELAY BOX

POWER CABLE

HEATER

Built-ins for the Bath

A few tricks with wood can make a bathroom more convenient and appealing. By boxing in an old-fashioned claw-footed bathtub or providing steps to a tub, you can give it a modern look. By adding a shelf to a vanity, storage is made more convenient. The right kind of wood, correctly installed, will readily survive the bathroom's damp environment.

Building these additions involves mostly routine carpentry plus some special attention to fastening and fitting. Wood additions to bathroom fixtures must be firmly anchored to the floor or the wall since there is no easy way to attach wood to the rim of a tub or a sink. Nailing or screwing through ceramic tile, the material most likely to be encountered in a bathroom, requires only a little extra care in drilling holes through the brittle tiles. The wood should fit snugly to the fixture and careful caulking is essential wherever wood meets a wall, the floor or the edges of fixtures to keep water from seeping in behind the wood structure.

Use exterior or marine-type plywood. Treat all exposed surfaces with one of the standard wood preservatives. For most sheathing ¼-inch plywood will do but use ¾ inch for any structures, such as steps, that are likely to bear much weight. After a framework has been attached and sheathed, it can be painted or covered with tile, plastic laminate or carpeting to match its surroundings.

Building steps to a tub involves many of the same techniques as framing around a tub. To turn the steps into spacesaving cabinets, you can build a glide-mounted drawer (page 51) into each step, converting the risers into drawer fronts.

Enclosing a Tub

1 **Building the frames.** Nail together a frame of 2-by-4s like that below for each side of the tub that is to be covered. Space the interior vertical studs of the frame about 16 inches apart. In designing the frame to fit under the lip of a lipped tub, or flush with the top of a non-lipped tub, allow for the thickness of a ½-inch board around the top of the frame (Step 3, overleaf) and of any finishing material you will attach to the top surface of the frame.

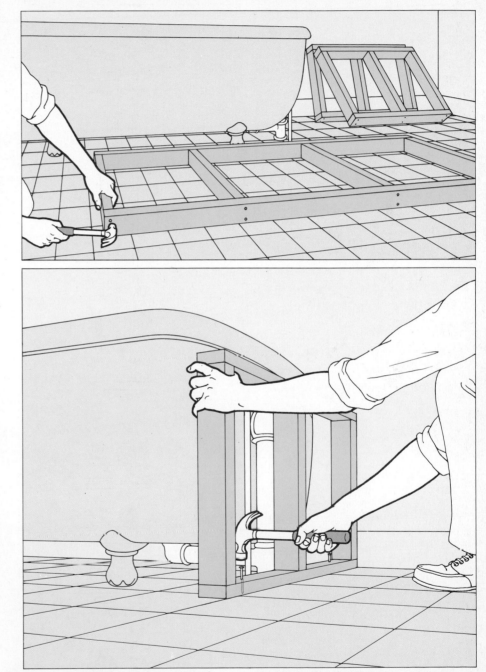

2 **Attaching the frames.** Drive 16-penny nails barely through the bottom 2-by-4 of the frame in the middle of each space between studs. Set the frame in place alongside the tub. Tap each nail enough to nick the tile beneath. Remove the frame and drill through the tiles at each mark with a carbide-tipped bit slightly larger than the nails. Run silicone seal along the bottom outside edge of the frame, reposition the frame and nail it to the floor through the holes in the tiles. At corners, nail the end braces together. Where an end brace meets a wall, attach it with toggle bolts, or, if the end brace abuts a stud, with nails.

3 **Attaching the top boards.** Cover the top surface of the frame with ½-inch boards nailed to the top members of the frame. These top boards should fit under the lip of a lipped tub with room to spare for the finished surface.

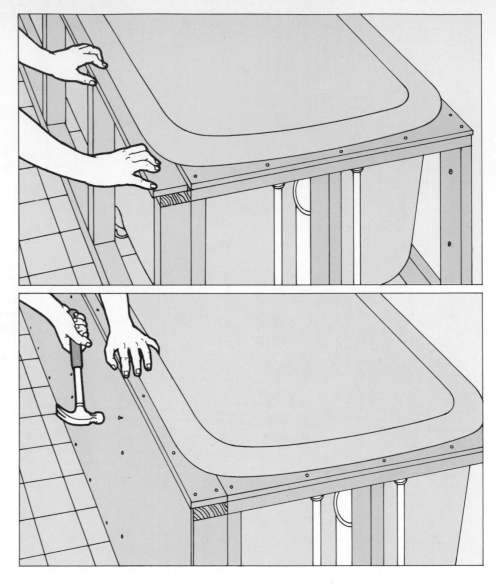

4 **Covering the frame.** Sheathe the outer sides of the frame with ¼-inch plywood fastened with galvanized nails. Leave a ⅟₁₆-inch space as an expansion joint where the edges of the sheathing meet the floor or a wall. If you cover the sheathing and the top boards with plastic laminate, use the techniques illustrated on pages 30-31; if with ceramic tile, those on pages 22-27. Caulk along the lines where the tub lip or the tub rim meets the finished top surface of the frame or where a top board meets the rim of a tub without a lip.

Adding Steps to a Tub

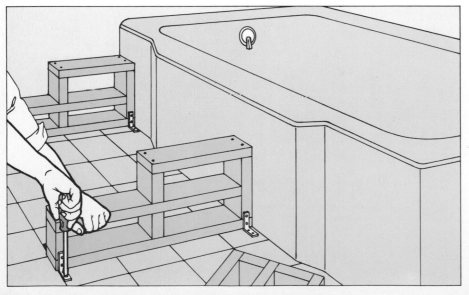

1 **Constructing the supports.** Build three frames of 2-by-4s as shown at left to support the steps. Use L-shaped metal brackets to fasten the supports to a tile floor screwing the brackets inside the end supports. Then nail on both risers, the bottom tread and side sheathing.

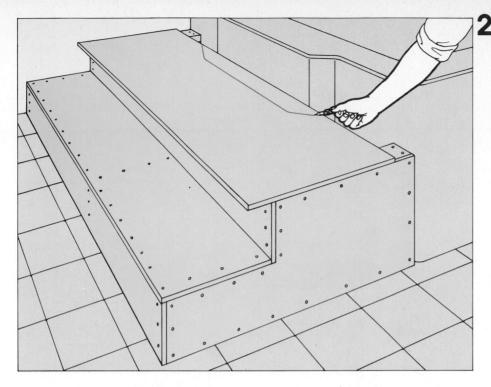

2 **Fitting the top tread.** To fit the top tread around a tub having a curved side, lay the tread on top of the supports against the midpoint of the side of the tub. Open a compass so it just covers the gap between the end of the tread and the end of the tub. Holding the pointed arm against the side of the tub, rest the pencil arm on the surface of the tread and guide the pointed arm along the tub side, following its curves *(left)*. Saw out the top tread along the pencil line, and nail it onto the supports. Cover or paint the steps and caulk along the lines where the steps meet the side of the tub.

Adding a Vanity Shelf

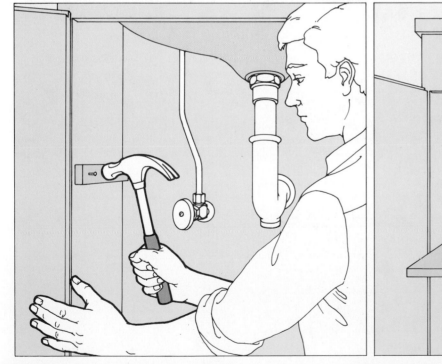

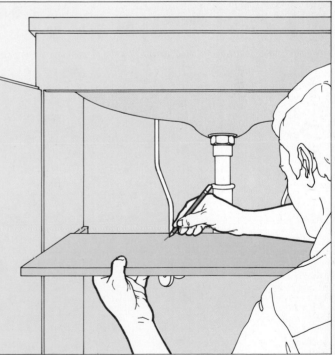

1 **Attaching cleats.** Use white glue or construction adhesive to secure two wood cleats, 1 by 2 inches, to the inside walls of a vanity. Light nails are handy to hold the cleats in place until the adhesive sets. Use a carpenter's level to make sure that the cleats are horizontal.

2 **Installing the shelf.** Place the shelf board on the cleats and slide it forward until it touches the drain. Mark the positions of the supply pipes and drainpipes *(above)*, and measure the distances from the front of the pipes to the back of the vanity. Mark the cutouts on the board, adding ¼ inch on each side for easy installation. Saw out the slots and slip the shelf into place.

Professional Techniques for Hanging Mirrors

Mounting mirrors requires care because they are heavy—up to 3⅓ pounds per square foot—awkward and fragile. Mirrors backed with hardboard (opposite, bottom) are easiest to work with because two or more steel hangers are riveted securely to the backing. These hangers are easily slipped over flat steel hooks that are screwed into the wall.

For an unbacked mirror use J clips—or flat steel hooks bent into a J shape—to support the bottom; L clips, plastic fasteners shaped like the letter L, hold the top of the mirror to the wall. Set small adhesive-backed pads, available at glass stores, behind the mirror to space it slightly away from the wall, so that raised places in the wall will not press against the fragile glass when you tighten the L clips. This small space also allows for the evaporation of trapped moisture.

Mirrors also can be attached to wallboard or plaster with construction adhesive. But this installation is permanent because the mirrors usually break during any attempted removal. Taking down a mirror hung properly with J and L clips is easy; simply unscrew the L clips while a helper holds the mirror back against the wall. Once the L clips are removed, the mirror can be tilted forward and then lifted off the supporting J clips. Some mirrors are mounted with screws that go through decorative plastic rosettes and then through holes drilled near the corners of the mirror. However, their use is becoming increasingly rare because drilling a mirror is a time-consuming and difficult task, which, like cutting one, is best left to a professional.

1 **Checking the wall.** Before hanging a mirror slide a straight board or level, longer than the mirror is wide, around the wall to see if it wobbles on a high spot. Irregularities of more than ⅛ inch call for extra padding (Step 3) on the back of the mirror's edge.

How to Move Glass Safely

Carrying a mirror. Carry a mirror vertically, never horizontally. You can support and maneuver it more easily and it will not tend to crack of its own weight. Keep your feet and legs out from under the mirror in case it falls—and if it does slip from your grasp, get out of the way. (Professionals call this "running away from the mirror.") Never attempt to catch a falling mirror.

A Mirror without a Backing

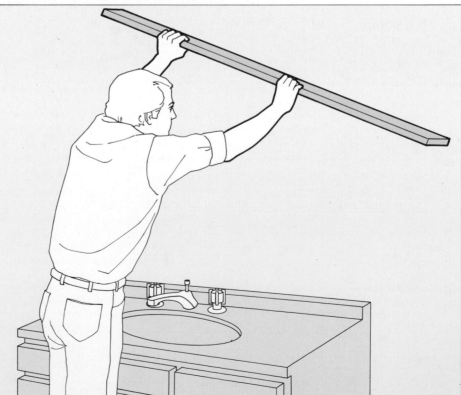

2 **Mounting J clips.** Using a level, mark a horizontal guideline as wide as the mirror for the bottom. Hold a steel J clip on this line at a point about one third of the distance from one end of the guideline. Drill a ³⁄₁₆-inch hole into the wall through each hole in the J clip. Put the clip aside and push in a 1-inch plastic anchor. Insert a 1-inch screw through the clip into the anchor. Repeat the procedure to mount a second clip one third of the distance from the other end of the line. Cover the screwheads with masking tape to prevent scratching the back of the mirror and line the inside of the J clips with felt or rubber. J-shaped tracks, sometimes preferred to J clips for esthetic reasons, mount in the same way.

3 **Setting the mirror.** Measure the height of the mirror and use a level to mark its side positions on the wall. One third of the distance down from the top of each line, and just to the outside, drill into the wall and insert a plastic anchor. Place adhesive-backed felt or rubber pads on the back of the mirror a third of the way down each side; if the wall is bowed, two or three pads may have to be stacked to keep the mirror from contacting the high spots. With a helper, angle the bottom of the mirror into the J clips. Tilt it to the wall and screw the L clips into the anchors. They should be tightened sufficiently to secure the mirror, but not so tight as to grind the glass back against the wall.

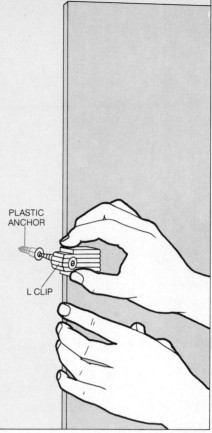

PLASTIC ANCHOR

L CLIP

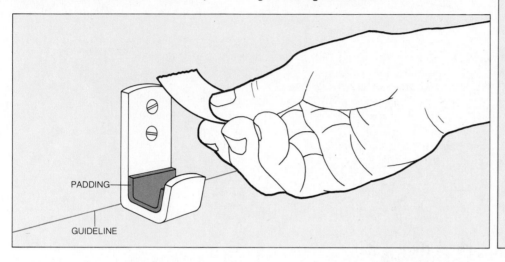

PADDING

GUIDELINE

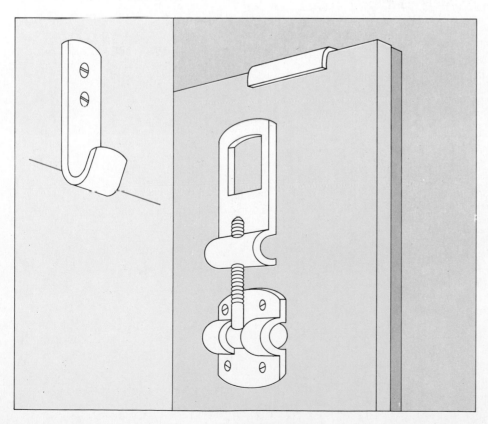

A Mirror with a Hardboard Backing

Hanging a backed mirror. Measure up from the bottom of the mirror to the top of the hole in one of the hangers riveted to the back of a backed mirror. Draw a bottom guideline as in Step 2 and measure up from it to draw a second line for the placement of the mirror hooks. Position flat metal hooks on the line and screw them into plastic anchors (far left). If your mirror has adjustable hangers, such as the ones shown at left, you can correct positioning errors with a few turns of the hanger. If the hangers are not adjustable, you can hook small turnbuckles onto the hooks and fasten the hangers to them, but be sure to allow for their length when positioning the hooks.

Tools for planning. Fixing the position of a toilet, perhaps the most crucial step in planning a new bathroom, starts with a floor plan, most easily sketched on graph paper. It need not be artfully drawn but measurements must be precise to locate such openings as the one for the toilet flange (center), on which the toilet will rest. The flange serves as a template for a rough tracing of the toilet drain outlet on the unfinished floor.

Nobody invented the modern kitchen and bathroom. Both rooms just grew over the past century and a half as American manufacturers began to mass-produce the devices that make them functional: cooking ranges, sinks, refrigerators, showers. Some of these essential fixtures—the bathtub and flush toilet, for instance—were ancient but so rare that ordinary people did not even know of their existence; others, like the microwave oven, are products of space-age technology. New or old, the operation of the fixtures has proved to be less a problem than the task of arranging them within a room. Where you place stove and sink, refrigerator and dishwasher, bathtub and vanity may have more effect on the usefulness, convenience and attractiveness of a kitchen or bathroom than the design of the fixtures themselves. As a result, planning the job, whether you are remodeling an existing room or building an entirely new one, is as important as the mechanics of installing pipes and appliances.

While minor improvements in layout can be made whenever fixtures are changed, the best opportunity obviously comes when you undertake major remodeling or start to build a kitchen or bathroom where none existed before. Then you can take advantage of research showing how to minimize the cook's work in a kitchen and of practical experience showing how to place fixtures to minimize the plumber's work in running pipes.

But while this background of knowledge may suggest an ideal layout, other factors may limit your ability to achieve the ideal. One is cost, of course; almost any layout desired is possible in a big room, but space is expensive and therefore scarce in modern homes. Another obstacle is legal—the various codes that regulate plumbing, wiring and house structure. But the house itself generally exerts the greatest influence on what you can do; existing plumbing and walls largely determine where fixtures can be placed and where new kitchens and bathrooms can be constructed, and unless you adapt your plans to the structure you have, remodeling or adding on becomes almost as big a job as building an entirely new house.

For most people, the first problem to be faced in planning a kitchen or bathroom is space. Generally, there is too little to provide for all desired uses. But in some old houses, there is so much that it may be wasted or distributed inconveniently. In both cases, different solutions apply to kitchen and bathroom.

The big bathroom is generally easy to improve by subdividing it *(page 87)*. The small bathroom suffers severe restrictions imposed by the sizes of fixtures. The minimum space for a full bathroom containing a standard tub, toilet and lavatory is 5 by 7 feet, but even in this minimum, a number of layouts are possible *(pages 85-86)*. And bathrooms can be fitted into smaller places by using scaled-down fixtures. A 30-by-42-inch square tub takes up less than 9 square feet of floor space, compared to 12½ square feet for the standard model. With a corner-mounted washbasin and toilet, you can squeeze a powder room into a total area of 4 square feet.

Miniaturized appliances are also available for kitchens. There are refrigerators 18 inches wide and 34 inches high, designed to fit underneath a counter; sinks 9 by 9 inches; and prefabricated units, 24 inches wide, that include a refrigerator, two-burner cook top and small sink. While such small devices are useful for an extra cooking area in a family room or private apartment, most kitchens require full-sized appliances, and the planning focuses on arranging them for maximum convenience while still providing space for all the other purposes the room must serve—as a place for family dining, homework and socializing.

Some solutions to these problems have been worked out by research performed after World War II, principally at Cornell University, which subjected the housewife's chores to the detailed time-and-motion studies previously applied to factory work. By filming women preparing meals, Cornell researchers discovered that as many as 252 trips to the refrigerator, the sink, the range and the mixing counter were needed to prepare dinner; just to throw together breakfast in some households took over 40 such trips. The researchers also found that more trips were made between sink and range than between refrigerator and mixing counter. The conclusions were obvious. Arranging the appliances so that they lie in a work triangle within easy reach of one another—sink and range closest to each other—and removing obstacles such as kitchen tables in the path between them results in faster, less fatiguing kitchen work. These findings have provided the basis for the layout of almost all kitchens today.

The Cornell studies also showed that in the average kitchen, the cook is alone only 50 per cent of the time, establishing that even modern "efficient" kitchens are more than simply food-preparation centers. By applying these results as shown on pages 80-83, you can design almost any kitchen to take full advantage of all the available space—gaining both a streamlined work area and enough room for informal dining and family gatherings.

While efficiency research and fixture designs suggest ideal plans for kitchen and bathroom, the realities of house structure and legal codes determine what is feasible. Plumbing is the principal limitation. Every house has at least one plumbing stack *(pages 78-79)*—in an economically built house there will be only one—a "tree" of branching pipes along which all fixtures of kitchen, bath and laundry are strung, taking their water supplies from its small pipes and emptying their wastes into its large ones. Any changes you plan should take into account the existing stack, for adding new branches to it is easier than installing an entirely new tree. A new stack is often practical, however, particularly if the house has rooms or closets that provide space for hiding large drains.

How the fixtures can be set along a stack, new or old, is spelled out in the several codes that regulate construction in most localities. Nearly all codes permit amateurs to do most (but not necessarily all) of the work on their own homes, provided they get permits and arrange for inspections. Although code requirements vary from place to place—often in seemingly capricious fashion—they generally are based on a sound rationale. By requiring techniques and materials that suit local needs, they guide you toward a safe and durable job.

Four different codes may affect work on a kitchen or bathroom: The building code regulates structural changes. In most communities, you must take out a permit to remove a bearing wall or to tamper with an exterior wall—whether building an addition or simply adding a new window or blocking off an old door. Some codes also require permits for less complex work, such as adding or removing a nonbearing partition. To apply for a building permit, you must submit a plan of the room to the local building inspector. The plan need not be elaborate, but it should be drawn to scale and indicate the location and sizes of existing doors and windows, the proposed location of new walls, doors or windows, and whether or not any wall you intend to remove is load bearing.

The mechanical code regulates work on heating and cooling systems, such as extending ductwork and removing radiators. Mechanical codes may also govern the installation of vent fans and range hoods and the installation or relocation of such appliances as gas ranges. For a mechanical permit, you also need a plan, one indicating details of furnace, air conditioner and distribution system.

The plumbing and electrical codes regulate those specialities and may require plans—for plumbing the plan is called a riser diagram—showing both the existing installation and the proposed changes. In some communities, an amateur can get an electrical permit only after passing a simple test of his knowledge of electrical techniques.

Applying for permits can be time consuming, so investigate your community's regulations well before you begin work. Copies of codes are available through the building department or at local libraries. Find out what plans are required and how many copies of each you will need to submit (some inspectors require as many as four sets). And check on the way inspections are handled in your area. Generally two are needed for each permit. The first takes place after all rough-in work has been done—ducts, wiring and pipes in place but not connected to appliances and fixtures, and walls framed but not closed. If each inspector approves the rough-in work, you are given permission to finish the walls and hook up appliances and fixtures. Then there is a final inspection of the finished work.

Finding the Best Pathways for the Piping

Remodeling a kitchen or bathroom, or installing a new one, is a major job that requires major planning. Before you turn the first screw or hammer the first nail, you must make basic decisions about the sizes and styles of fixtures and appliances, clearances, floor and wall coverings, lighting, heating and ventilation. Most important of all, you must decide upon the routes of new plumbing lines (right). The location of existing plumbing and the distance it can be moved—or whether it can be moved at all—will often dictate the layout of a remodeled kitchen or bathroom, and may limit your choice of locations for a new one.

In most homes, plumbing fixtures are clustered around a vertical core of supply pipes and drainpipes. A bathroom is often located above or behind the kitchen, or over a basement utility room. Each plumbing fixture in these rooms must be supplied with hot and cold water from parallel lines that run through the core. Waste water and sewage are carried away from the fixtures by branch drains that run to the soil stack—a large, vertical drain dropping down to the main house drain. Each fixture has a drain trap that prevents sewer gases from entering the house. And each has a vent pipe that exhausts waste gases through a chimney-like stack and admits fresh air to the drains, maintaining the pressure behind the flow of drain water and wastes, and preventing water from being siphoned out of the traps.

Roughing-in, the job of installing plumbing where none exists, involves running new piping through the walls, floors and ceilings. Because drainpipes and vent pipes—collectively called the drain-waste-vent, or DWV, system—are the most complicated part of a plumbing network, they are always planned and installed (pages 104-111) before the supply lines. Drains work by gravity: they are large (1½ to 4 inches in diameter), and must be pitched on horizontal runs and kept as straight as possible. The location

of drainpiping is rigidly governed by plumbing codes. If their location exceeds a specified "critical distance" from an existing vent (page 108), you must install a new vent—and in some circumstances you may have to add an entire vent and drain stack, as in Room 3 in the drawing.

Extending supply pipes usually poses fewer problems. They are relatively small (½ to ¾ inch in diameter) and can be elbowed into sharp turns. But added fixtures can reduce water flow through the supply lines in a system that already has low pressure or constricted pipes. If you have these problems, investigate possible remedies (pages 115-117) before planning plumbing additions.

Concealing new pipes, especially the large drainpipes, can be tricky. If the new kitchen or bathroom is over a crawl space or an unfinished basement, horizontal pipes can easily be run between or beneath the floor joists. For a new installation above a finished ceiling, you must cut away part of the ceiling to install the pipes and you may have to drill or notch joists to accommodate them. There are limits on where and how deeply you can cut a joist (pages 101-103); in some cases, you may have to run the pipes below the ceiling, and then conceal them.

Vertical pipes are usually concealed inside a framed structure called a wet wall, substantially thicker than an ordinary partition and created by furring out an existing wall (page 96) or building an entirely new one (pages 97-99). Alternatively, pipes can be run alongside an existing wall and concealed—in cabinets, bookcases, closets or specially made paneling.

Electrical lines for a new bathroom or kitchen pose fewer problems than new plumbing lines. Electrical cable is flexible and can easily be snaked through walls and ceilings (pages 52-53); the new lines can be powered from existing outlet boxes or directly from the service panel. Ducts are bulkier, but usually not difficult to run: the fans for bathroom ceilings or kitchen range hoods (pages 56-59) are

usually vented through lengths of duct run to the outside through the roof or sides of the house.

Since plumbing pipes, electrical lines and vent ducts may have to run over long distances, route them in the same direction if you can to minimize the cutting and patching of walls and ceilings. This part of the planning job is tricky. For example, if you plan to expand a room by removing a wall (pages 94-95), be sure that you will not endanger the house structure or disrupt vital services.

First determine whether the wall is load bearing (page 60)—almost all outside walls are. Then find out what services the wall contains. Electrical switches or outlets indicate wiring that must be removed or relocated. Heating registers are signs of ducts, which can be rerouted but generally not removed. In some cases, a duct can be cut back and capped with a floor register. Ducts that cannot be cut back or rerouted must be left in place and concealed with drywall or paneling to match the remodeled room.

The presence of plumbing fixtures along a wall, or along a corresponding wall in the room directly above, indicates pipes within the wall that must be moved. If the plumbing ends at the existing fixtures (you may have to cut a small hole in the wall to check its route), it can be removed and capped (page 93). Supply pipes and small branch drains passing through the wall to fixtures above can usually be rerouted. But large drains and soil stacks usually must be left in place and concealed.

Once you know where you can best place the new services, make a floor plan of the room, indicating the locations and dimensions for walls, doors, windows, and plumbing and electrical outlets. Follow the plan as closely as you can in every step of the remodeling process, from running plumbing and electrical lines to arranging fixtures and appliances—and even to ordering and cutting new wall and floor coverings.

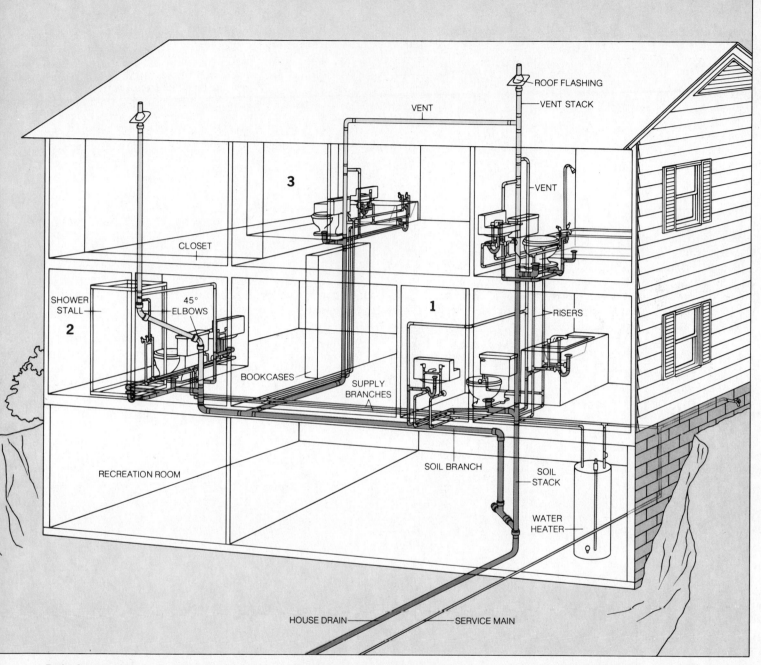

ROOF FLASHING

VENT — VENT STACK

VENT

VENT

3

CLOSET

SHOWER
STALL

45°
ELBOWS

RISERS

2

BOOKCASES

1

SUPPLY
BRANCHES

RECREATION ROOM

SOIL BRANCH

SOIL
STACK

WATER
HEATER

HOUSE DRAIN — SERVICE MAIN

Paths for new pipes. In this two-story house, the existing plumbing core consists of two systems of pipes running from the basement to a first-floor kitchen and a second-floor bathroom. Supply pipes (*blue*) carry cold water from the service main and hot water from the water heater. Drains (*green*) and vents (*yellow*) run to a soil stack that vents gases through the roof and carries wastes down to the main drain.

Three new installations—a powder room next to the kitchen and full baths on the first and second floors—illustrate ways in which new plumbing can be added to an existing system.

1 Powder room. All the newly installed fixtures are close enough to the existing plumbing core to be tied directly into it. A new drain runs across the open ceiling underneath the powder room to the existing stack, and a new vent is connected to the existing vent. The supply lines are short extensions of nearby hot and cold vertical lines, called risers.

2 First-floor bathroom. Supply branches and a soil branch (the large horizontal drain) run across the basement ceiling to and from the new bathroom. The pipes that cross the finished ceiling in the recreation room can be concealed

by a soffit or a dropped ceiling. The vent, too far from the existing vent for a direct connection, is a new vent, offset with 45° elbows to carry it into the closet of a second-floor bedroom and onto a new roof outlet.

3 Second-floor bath. An even larger run of supply piping and drainpiping runs to the second floor across the length and width of the basement and up along a first-floor wall, where it is concealed by floor-to-ceiling bookcases. The vent, however, is close enough to the existing stack to be connected to it by a pipe running up through the wall and across the attic.

Basing a Kitchen on a Step-saving Triangle

To prepare two meals—breakfast and dinner—a family cook walks 120 miles a year. As much as a third of this mileage may be waste motion, inflicted upon the cook by appliances placed not for efficiency but for economy in construction. In an efficient kitchen, three "activity centers" focused at the refrigerator, the sink and the range lie within easy reach of the cook—and according to a study made at Cornell University, better placement of these activity centers can eliminate as much as 40 miles a year from the kitchen marathon.

A kitchen that, whatever its shape and size, is designed for efficient use rather than construction economies, has its major fixtures and appliances in one of the four basic layouts shown on pages 82-83: the U, the L, the corridor and the one-wall. In each layout, the three activity centers make up the three points of a work triangle, and in an efficient kitchen the sides of the triangle add up to no more than 23 feet. Up to a point, the smaller the triangle the greater the efficiency; its minimum size is dictated by the need for working space—each activity center must have a minimum of counter area and storage volume (right and on page 82). Avoid layouts that route household traffic through the work triangle, and allow at least 48 inches between facing base cabinets or appliances—enough space to allow you to stand at an open cabinet, refrigerator or oven while another person edges past.

The sink is the main activity center, accounting for 40 to 46 per cent of all kitchen work time. Ideally, it belongs at the center of the work triangle, within 4 to 6 feet of the range and 4 to 7 feet of the refrigerator. Locate the dishwasher within 12 inches of the sink, for convenient loading and the simplest pattern of plumbing connections, but do not set the dishwasher at right angles to the sink—in this arrangement you will have to move away from the sink every time you open the dishwasher door.

A single-bowl sink is adequate for a kitchen with a dishwasher; use a double-bowl model if you plan to wash and rinse dishes by hand. In a double sink, at least one of the bowls should be large enough for a roasting pan—that is, a pan at least 20 inches long.

The range is the cooking and serving center, best located for easy access to the dining area. It is also the spot at which most kitchen injuries occur. Avoid an arrangement in which people passing through the kitchen are likely to brush against the range, and never place a range under a window: grease-laden curtains can blaze up easily, and you must reach across the burners to open and close the window. Wall cabinets over the range should be at least 30 inches above the cook-top surface, and the counter surface next to the range should have heat-resistant areas for hot pots and pans.

In a large kitchen you may want a separate oven and range. An oven is the least used of all major kitchen appliances—it accounts for less than 10 per cent of the trips to and from the activity centers and can lie outside the work triangle without a significant loss of efficiency. The bottom of a wall oven should be 3 inches below elbow height, a level that minimizes the chance of burning an arm on an oven rack and is comfortable for turning or basting food.

Locate a refrigerator at the end of a counter, where it will not cut counter space into several small, cramped work areas. Get a refrigerator with hinges away from the counter, so that the open door will not block work space—many modern models have doors adjustable to open either way. To dissipate the heat of the condenser coils at the back of a refrigerator, allow at least 3 inches between the top of the unit and any overhanging cabinets, and 1 to 2 inches between the side and an adjoining wall or broom closet. Models with top-mounted coils can be more snugly enclosed.

Any of the three activity centers can be located in a kitchen island or peninsula, but islands are seldom practical in average kitchens because they need at least 5 feet of floor space on one of their long sides and at least 3 feet along their short ones. Even though you have adequate space for an island, avoid using it for the range or the main sink: both centers need more counter space than most island installations permit.

In practice, the counter space for an activity center may vary considerably from the dimensions recommended in the plans opposite and on page 82, top. In a limited space two activity centers can share counter space, but try to keep a shared counter at least as long as the most generous minimum length for the two centers, plus 1 foot. And at some point in the assembly (usually between the refrigerator and sink) try to keep at least 36 inches of counter space for a mixing and food-preparation center.

A large kitchen permits more variations, but has one paradoxical limitation: Try not to exceed the maximum recommended dimensions of the plans. Extra counter space means extra steps between work centers—and extra work for the cook.

The Three Activity Centers

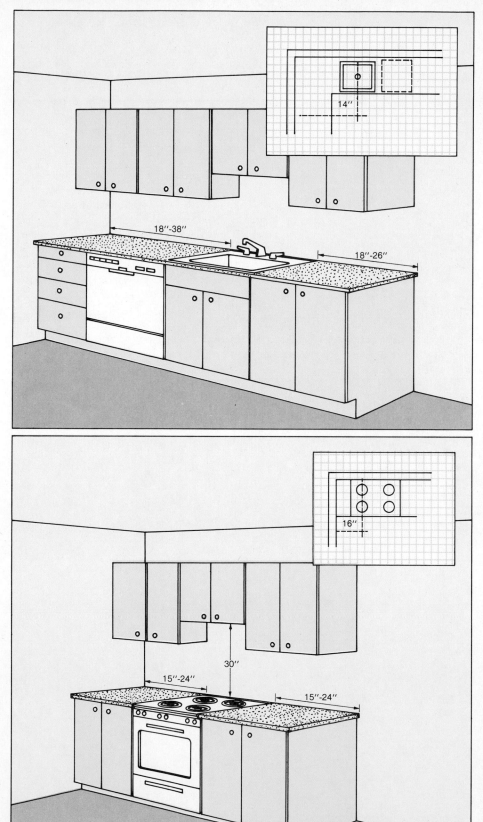

The sink. Provide at least 18 inches of counter space on each side of the sink. If more space is available, add 6 or 8 inches of countertop on one side for preparing food and stacking un-washed dishes, and from 10 to 20 inches on the other for draining and stacking washed dishes. A dishwasher next to a sink will have at least 24 inches of counter space above it. For a sink near a corner *(inset)*, allow at least 14 inches be-tween the sink center line and the corner.

The range. Allow at least 15 inches of counter space beside the range for resting pots and setting out serving dishes, or up to 24 inches on each side if space allows. For a range next to a wall or another appliance *(inset)*, allow a safety margin of at least 16 inches from the center of the nearest burner. A range with less than 10 inches between burners must have at least 10 inches of counter space on each side, so that pot handles will not jut into the work area.

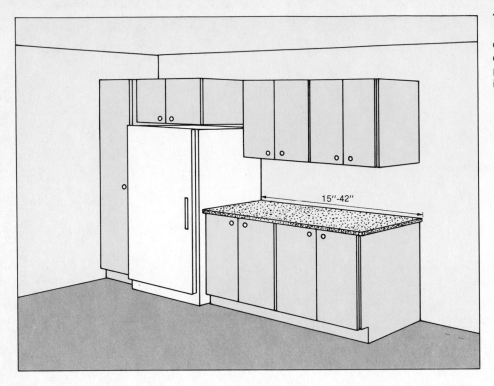

The refrigerator center. Provide at least 15 inches of counter space on the latch side of the refrigerator for setting out supplies. If this counter must also form part of the food-preparation center, provide between 36 and 42 inches of uninterrupted counter space.

15"-42"

The Four Layouts

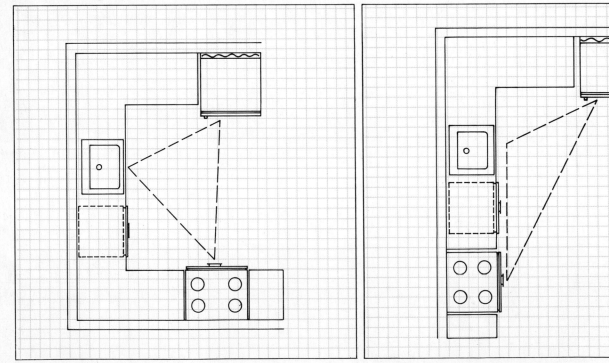

The U. Cabinets and counters set along three walls keep the three activity centers accessible to one another and out of the way of traffic. The back wall should measure between 8 and 13 feet, allowing from 4 to 9 feet of work area between facing counters—a tighter arrangement makes for cramped work areas; a looser one, too many steps between activity centers.

The L. This adaptable plan is best for small square kitchens; in large ones it provides a work triangle isolated from traffic and frees the rest of the room for dining. Its drawbacks are the long distance between two of the work centers and the need for expensive corner cabinets. Arrange the centers with a sink in the middle, creating a refrigerator-to-sink-to-range work flow.

The corridor. In this arrangement, usually found in a kitchen that also serves as a passageway, appliances and cabinets are distributed along two facing walls. Because the work triangle will be broken by traffic, try to locate the range and the sink—the most active work centers—along the same wall. The corridor aisle should be at least 4 feet wide to provide adequate clearance between cabinet and appliance doors. If your aisle is narrower, try to stagger the three work centers so that appliance doors do not interfere with one another.

The one-wall. This layout works best in an area less than 12 feet long; if the arrangement is strung out to gain more cabinets and larger counters, the distances between work centers become too large for efficiency. Use scaled-down appliances to provide maximum counter and cabinet space, and save steps by locating the refrigerator at one end, the range at the other and the sink in between, with most of the counter space between the sink and the range.

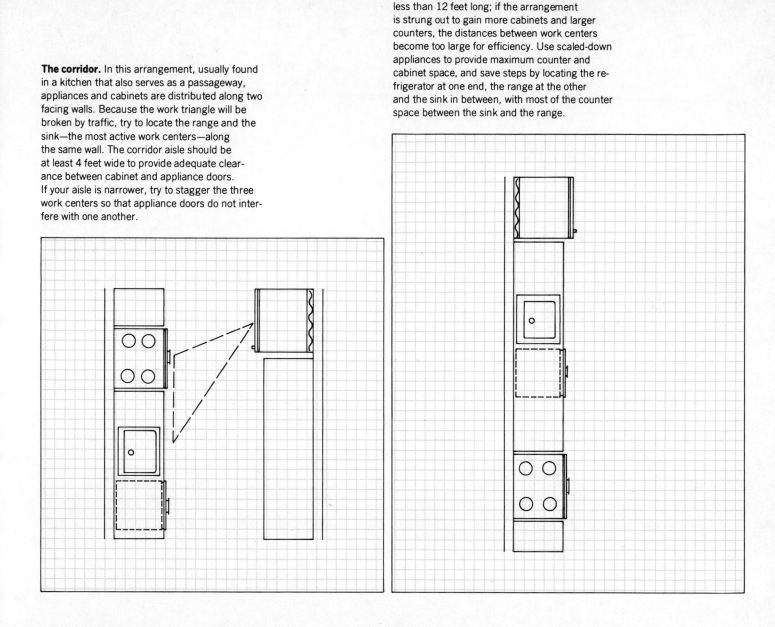

Making a Dangerous Room Safer

According to the National Safety Council, about a fourth of all serious home accidents take place in the kitchen. The placement of appliances and the arrangement of work spaces shown on these pages reduce or eliminate many hazards, but designers and safety experts also recommend safety measures for specific danger points.

☐ Choose a kitchen range that has controls at the front or sides, not at the back of the burners.

☐ Hang a dry chemical fire extinguisher especially designed for grease fires within easy reach of the range—but do not hang it directly above the cook top, where you might have to reach through flames to get at it.

☐ Hang kitchen doors so that they swing out of the room rather than into the work triangle.

☐ Locate hanging or wall-mounted light fixtures at least 6 feet 8 inches above the floor, unless they hang over

an island, a base cabinet or a table.

☐ Install a ground-fault interrupter *(page 55)* to protect receptacles at or near a sink. (However, note that a GFI cannot be used in the split 240-volt circuits shown on page 54; it is intended only for ordinary 120-volt circuits.)

☐ Isolate the storage areas of dangerous tools and chemicals. Store your sharp knives and choppers separately from other utensils, and store cleaning products separately from food.

Bathrooms to Fit the Space

Bathrooms are usually the smallest rooms in a house—and even a large bathroom has a way of seeming inadequate when every member of the family wants it at once. You may be able to use the space more efficiently by adding a second washbowl or partitioning off a toilet; in some situations, you can enlarge a bathroom by removing a wall and picking up a few feet from an adjoining room or closet. But the most satisfactory solution to the problem is another bathroom—a new one, built into whatever space you find available. A full bathroom with standard fixtures can fit into a space 5 by 7 feet, a half bath (toilet and sink) into a space as small as 4 feet square.

In such small rooms, the fixtures must be placed with special care to provide minimum clearances at the front and sides. (Most building codes specify these clearances; if your local code does not, use the diagrams at right as a guide.) At the same time, the layout of the bathroom is influenced by the location of existing plumbing or the routes of new pipes. Juggling the positions of your fixtures to meet both requirements calls for ingenuity and patience.

In a room with an existing soil stack or one in which a new stack must be located in a particular area, position the toilet first—it must be near the stack. Try to locate the toilet next to a wall, for convenience in mounting a toilet-paper holder, but remember that some people find the sight of a toilet from an open door objectionable: always face a toilet away from a door if you can, and if the space is available consider separating the toilet from the other fixtures with a partition.

Because a full bathtub is very heavy, the floor joists under the tub must have extra bracing (page 102) and the best location is along a wall or in a corner. Position the foot of the tub against a wall that can be opened from the other side for plumbing repairs.

The lavatory is the most frequently used fixture. Place it well away from the tub and toilet, with space around it for towel racks and hooks, toothbrush racks and cabinets or storage shelves. In a windowed bathroom, try to give the lavatory the advantage of natural light for shaving and applying make-up.

When you have chosen the locations of these three fixtures, use the manufacturer's rough-in dimensions to plan the connections of each fixture to its plumbing. Mark the rough-in points on the walls and floors of the room (some fixtures come with rough-in templates that you can tack or tape to walls and floors), then decide upon the routes of the pipes to and from the rough-in points. The details of the routes will depend on the floor plan, the location of existing plumbing and the requirements of your local plumbing code. Three of the most common fixture arrangements, with progressively more complicated plumbing, are shown in the floor plans at right and on page 86. The plans are for the smallest practical rooms, but the plumbing patterns will also serve large bathrooms and additional fixtures (page 87).

In any small bathroom, new or old, you will confront the problem of getting adequate storage and counter space. Some simple solutions:

☐ Mount shallow shelves along a wall behind the door.

☐ Set the hinges on the door so that it swings outward.

☐ Replace a wall-mounted or pedestal lavatory with a vanity that provides both counter space and an enclosed cabinet beneath the washbowl.

☐ Extend a vanity top over the top of the toilet tank—use a removable extension, so that you can get to the tank for repairs.

☐ Use the space above the toilet as a storage wall.

☐ Build shelves or cabinets into the spaces between studs (pages 60-63).

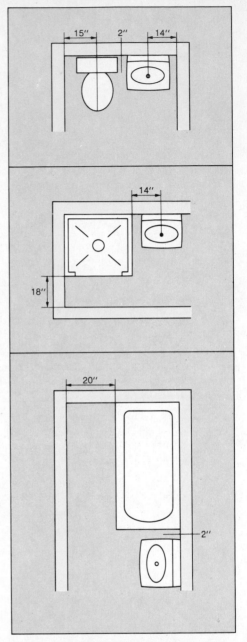

Minimum fixture clearances. For the average adult, the clearances indicated in the floor plans above are the minimums for using standard bathroom fixtures and cleaning around them. Minimum clearances mean minimal comfort: exceed the figures if you can. A 14-inch clearance between the center line of a lavatory and a wall, for example, allows barely enough room to shave or apply make-up; 18 inches between a shower and a wall allows only enough room to edge out of the shower. When a toilet and a lavatory or tub face each other, 18 inches between them provides no more than knee room in front of the toilet and just enough room to stand in front of the lavatory or to towel off beside the tub. Most bathroom designers—and some municipal codes—specify 24-inch minimum clearances for comfortable use of these fixtures.

Rough-in dimensions. Make large, clear, rough-in marks on walls and floors for pipe-to-fixture connections, with the centers of pipe holes indicated precisely. The dimensions shown here are typical for U.S. and Canadian fixtures (your own may be slightly different). They match the plumbing pattern shown at right, below.

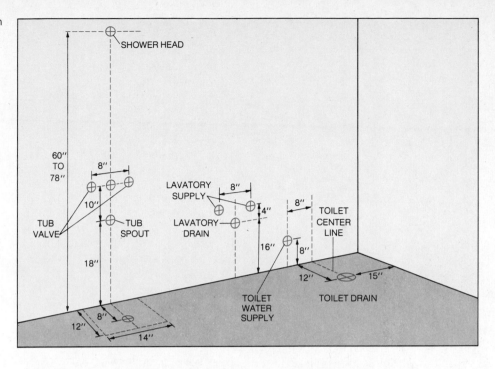

SHOWER HEAD

60" TO 78"

8"

TUB VALVE

10"

TUB SPOUT

18"

8"

12"

14"

LAVATORY SUPPLY

8"

LAVATORY DRAIN

4"

16"

8"

8"

TOILET WATER SUPPLY

12"

TOILET CENTER LINE

TOILET DRAIN

15"

Three Basic Plumbing Patterns

One wall. The simplest bathroom for a limited space has fixtures in a row, with all their plumbing in a single wall. This arrangement calls for the least amount of cutting into the house structure and uses the fewest fittings.

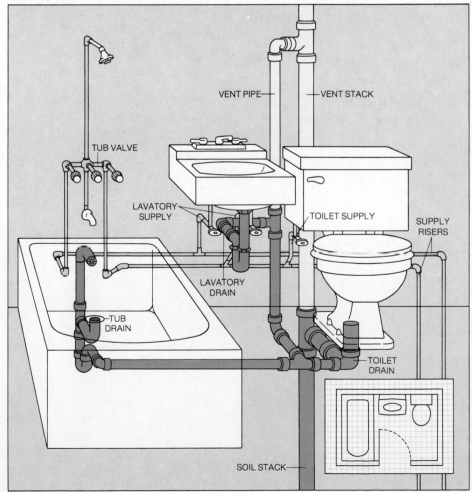

VENT PIPE

VENT STACK

TUB VALVE

LAVATORY SUPPLY

TOILET SUPPLY

SUPPLY RISERS

LAVATORY DRAIN

TUB DRAIN

TOILET DRAIN

SOIL STACK

Two walls. A bathroom with plumbing in two adjoining walls provides somewhat more storage and activity space around the lavatory than a one-wall room, and the plumbing is only slightly more complicated. But a two-wall bathroom generally requires more cutting of studs and joists to accommodate the pipes; to minimize cutting or, as here, to clear a door, try to run the supply lines underneath or between joists rather than through the walls.

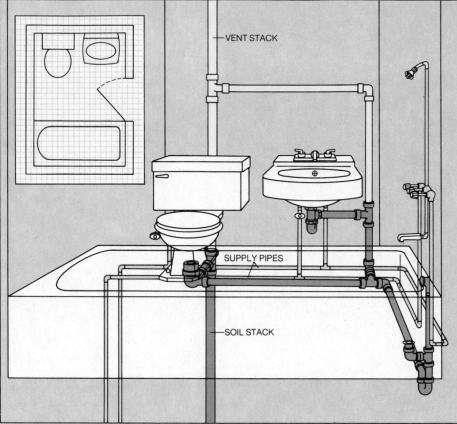

Three walls. Of all the basic bathroom plans, this offers the greatest flexibility and the largest wall and counter spaces—at the cost of added room area and more complex plumbing. The room must be at least 5½ feet by 7 feet 2 inches to accommodate minimum clearances between fixtures; in practice, three-wall bathrooms are usually set up in larger rooms—at least 7 feet 8 inches by 6 feet. Venting is especially difficult. Your local code may require separate vents for each fixture, and even with the single lavatory vent shown here, a connection to the vent stack may be hard to make. If the space above the bathroom is unfinished, run the pipe diagonally across it. Otherwise, the vent must be run inside the room, boxed in a wallboard enclosure, or extended up to the attic or roof.

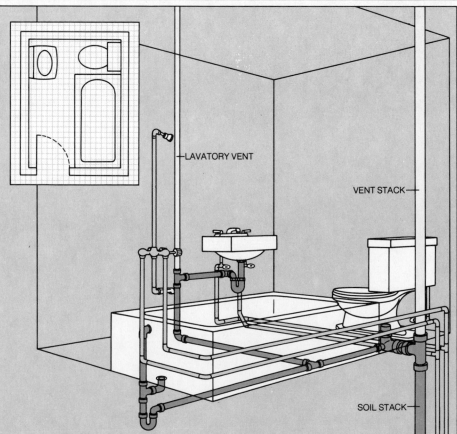

The Luxury That Size Allows

An expanded bathroom. Fixtures can be added to any of the basic bathroom plans with surprisingly little additional plumbing. For example, a 5-by-7-foot one-wall bathroom (*inset*) is expanded with a second toilet and a vanity, installed in what had been an adjoining closet.

In the illustration below, the old piping is shown in white, the new in color. The new fixtures drain into the stack through a new sanitary T (*page 104*) directly beneath the existing one. New drainpipes and supply pipes run horizontally beneath the floor to the new lavatory; the vertical

supply risers and the drain behind the lavatory could be concealed by furring out the original wall (*page 96*) or installing a new wet wall (*pages 97-99*). The lavatory vent could reach the vent stack by a route that runs around the room or up to the attic or roof.

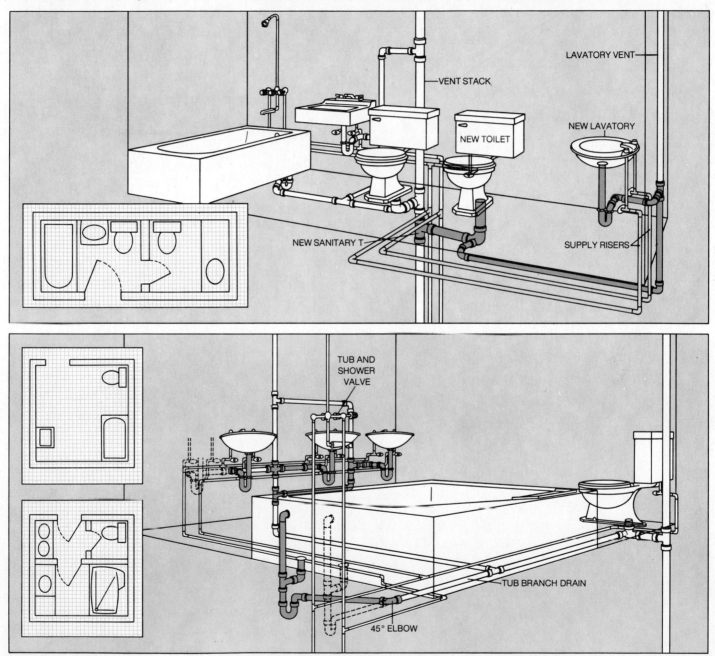

VENT STACK

LAVATORY VENT

NEW TOILET

NEW LAVATORY

NEW SANITARY T

SUPPLY RISERS

TUB AND SHOWER VALVE

TUB BRANCH DRAIN

45° ELBOW

A redesigned bathroom. Many older homes have very large bathrooms equipped with no more than a standard tub, a toilet and a standing lavatory. In a typical 10-by-11-foot room (*top inset*), the rest of the space is wasted. For maximum versatility, the room can be partitioned into functionally separate sections, with new doors

between them (*bottom inset*). The section nearest the original door becomes a powder room with double vanity sinks and an enclosed toilet. The inner section gets a new oversized tub, and a vanity sink and dressing table replace the old standing lavatory. The original plumbing (*white and dotted lines*) follows the plan of a

three-wall bathroom, with pipes concealed inside three wet walls. An elbow in the tub branch drain routes the drain to a point beneath the outlet of the new tub. The supply lines to the tub and shower valve are in their original positions; the new lavatories tie into the plumbing of the original single lavatory.

Adding Style to Efficiency

Of all the spaces in a modern home, kitchens and bathrooms are the most used and useful, the most expensively equipped and the most permanently arranged. Until recently, they were also the rooms in which least thought was given to decor, and the ones in which no one spent a minute longer than necessary. The emphasis was on compactness and efficiency. The look—white fixtures and appliances, slightly relieved by chrome spigots, spouts and trim—was that of an antiseptic laboratory.

No longer. Color has burst into both rooms, and a sense of style. Practicality and economy of space have not been forgotten, but these functional rooms have gained extra dimensions of attractiveness—partly from tasteful design, partly from coordination into the needs of family life.

The long neglect—and delayed renaissance—of kitchen and bathroom can be tied to history. The Romans had kitchens with efficient built-in stoves and under-the-floor drains; they raised bathing to the level of a communal occasion. The Emperor Caracalla is remembered today less for having murdered his brother than for the magnificent public baths constructed during his reign.

What happened in the centuries between the fall of Rome and the Industrial Revolution can be seen on a tour of any of the fine Colonial homes now preserved as museums. The visitor to an 18th Century mansion in the South will see gracious, airy entranceways, living rooms and bedrooms; only when he leaves does he realize he did not see a kitchen or a bathroom. For the rich, cooking was done by servants in an outbuilding or basement; the poor cooked in the room they lived—and often slept—in. No one, rich or poor, had a bathroom.

The Industrial Revolution changed that with mass production of cookstoves, iceboxes, tubs, toilets and all the paraphernalia that have become essential equipment in the modern household. The appliances demanded rooms of their own—but the appliances took over. The rooms provided were considered to be simply spaces in which the appliances were to be used: a bathroom was for getting clean, a kitchen for cooking. This trend was accelerated as homes became smaller, intensifying competition for space. The Roman idea that bathing could be enjoyable was forgotten, as was the frontier idea that the kitchen could be the sociable center of family life.

Those values are finally being rediscovered. Although few modern bathrooms rival Caracalla's, they are no longer mechanical assemblages of fixtures. Because a family wants flexibility and privacy in its bathrooms, tubs are separated from lavatories, lavatories from toilets—and hall closets become powder rooms. Ideally, a kitchen is not only a pleasant place to work, but also a living and entertainment center in which the working cook can share in other activities. In some houses the kitchen may flow into a living room, family room, sewing room, office—or even, given the right climate, the outdoors *(pages 88B-88C)*.

In a room that is small and must remain small, the designer's ingenuity meets its greatest challenge. For the kitchen, the simplest scheme is usually the best—a parallel arrangement of counters makes an attractive cooking area out of what seems to be a corridor *(page 88E)*. A small bathroom looks larger when it contains transparent elements or mirrored walls *(pages 88F-88G)*. What is most important, even the smallest kitchen or a closet-sized bathroom can be planned to look quite as colorful and inviting as any other room in your house.

A dual personality. This kitchen, fitted smoothly and economically into a corner of the living-dining area, allows the cook to work without being exiled from family activities and at the same time to keep pots, pans and dirty dishes in the background. Windows at the rear, offering an alternate outlook, provide the enclave with a personality of its own, and when not in use the kitchen blends gracefully into the general decor.

A

Kitchens to Live In

Human society presumably grew up around the cook fire, and kitchens were traditionally centers of sociability until the shrinking size of the American home drove everyone out but the cook. While she—always she—was working in that machine-crammed space, she was cut off from other activities in the house. Today the cook may be either husband or wife, and food preparation in isolation is no longer the rule. The kitchen in many homes once again has become the focus of family life.

No longer confined to a location that allows access only to the dining room, the modern kitchen lends itself to a variety of uses. A home office *(below)* is a common addition. A kitchen set at the center of things keeps host and hostess part of the party while the work necessary to entertaining goes on. And, if desired, a kitchen like the one at right can even be integrated into the outdoors.

An office for the kitchen. A small office more than earns its space in any kitchen by providing a nook where the cook can compose grocery lists, consult recipes, take care of bills or even write a novel while keeping an eye on the stew. In the kitchen at right, a minimum of space is cleverly compartmented to accommodate books, plants, a TV and a clutter-concealing fold-up desk. The made-to-order stained-glass window blocks an uninspiring view of a garage while adding an element of pure delight.

background, but the Mediterranean climate favors outdoor dining and entertainment, and the brick floor of the kitchen flows into a patio and onward to a large lawn.

At the heart of the house. The island kitchen below offers an ideal location for the cook who wants to be in on everything. Glass walls and broad archways connect it with the patio in the foreground, a dining room at left, a breakfast area at near right and the living room at far right.

The Compact Kitchen

Space in most households is one of the most precious of domestic resources and a well-planned kitchen can help to conserve it by fitting into whatever space is available. Imagination and the wide choice of equipment designed for limited spaces and odd corners can create a kitchen that combines compactness with utility and charm. Refrigerators nest under stoves; counters double as work surfaces and eating space; tables fold or slide out of the way when not in use. But, as shown here, even standard equipment thoughtfully laid out can make a small space roomy.

Planned to the last inch. This tiny kitchen has no space to spare, but efficient planning has left room for all the necessities, including generous storage space and ample work surfaces. The arrangement of appliances does double duty. Grouped on either side of the entrance, they are out of the way of the work area. They also help to create an illusion of additional space by forming a narrow entryway from which the rest of the room broadens out to the walls.

A traveling table. The round table in this London apartment can be used in the kitchen as a work surface or for family meals. For more formal dining, or when more space is needed in the kitchen, the table slides on casters through a slot in the wall into the living room. Above the table is a pass-through, equipped with sliding doors, for easy serving or for clearing the table.

A kitchen in a corridor. The ingenious arrangement above replaces the original basement kitchen of a New York brownstone. The owners partitioned off a slice of the living room and installed this corridor kitchen, complete with all appliances and with counters on both sides. The monochromatic color scheme, the straight lines of the floor-to-ceiling storage units and a mirror behind the sink make this shipshape passageway look larger than it really is.

The Adaptable Bathrooms

The bathroom seems the most intractable room in the house. It is usually allotted the least space, yet it must hold standardized, bulky fixtures.

Most bathrooms can be made far more useful by adding simple equipment, either store-bought or home-made *(right)*. The challenge, however, comes with the need for fitting a bathroom or powder room into minimum space. Small fixtures help. Mirrors *(opposite and below)* can enlarge the room visually. But careful placement and selection of standard materials make the real difference.

Extra room for laundry. In addition to its regular functions, this wood-paneled bathroom in England lends a hand with the laundry. A trap door in the ceiling lets down to reveal lines for hanging drip-dry clothing or wet towels above the tub.

Raising a family. A shelf adjustable to three different levels provides easy access to a washbasin and mirror for children of varying heights. The shelf rests on cleats firmly fastened to the wall and on slots in the framing around the tub.

Unlimited illusory space. The little powder room above was cleverly contrived within an odd corner of otherwise waste space in an old New York apartment. Mirrored walls endlessly repeating the streamlined curves of simple fixtures give a feeling of infinite space. The theatrical lighting adds a touch of glamor.

A see-through shower. The shower stall takes up a substantial chunk of space in this already tiny New York bathroom, but by replacing the conventional curtain with a plexiglass enclosure and by adding a striking cutout mural that flows around corners along the wall the owners have added both eye room and color.

F

Rich though small. The attention lavished on details gives this pocket-sized bathroom charm and importance. Marble wainscots the walls and encases the tub. The washbasin, faucet handles and even the soap dish repeat the ceiling pattern. Mirrors multiply the effect and give the feeling of being surrounded by a field of flowers.

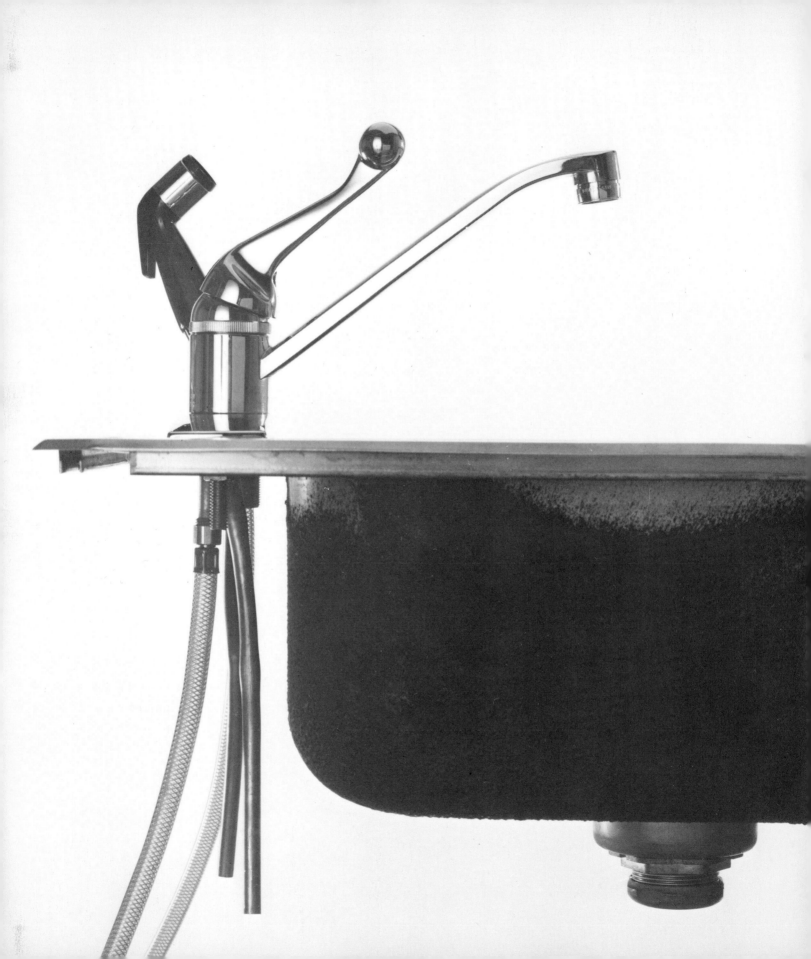

4 Plumbing for the New Rooms

Profile of a sink. Hidden beneath the gleam of the chrome fittings and stainless-steel bowl are the unglamorous parts involved in the installation of a new sink. The rim clamps the unit to the countertop. Extending down from the faucet assembly are built-in copper tubes that are connected to the house supply lines with compression fittings. The hose of the spray attaches to the faucet assembly with a similar fitting, and the drain connection under the sink is made with slip nuts.

Creating a new kitchen or bathroom is an undertaking that can be less formidable than it seems at first. The trick is to cut the job down. It may call for no more than the removal and replacement of old fixtures (pages 90-93) or, at a more ambitious level, the installation of new walls (pages 96-103). Use as much of the existing plumbing as you can. Where extensions are necessary, choose materials that are easy to work with; you do not have to match new plumbing materials to old because adapters make the transition. The easiest is plastic, light in weight, readily cut with a saw and assembled with cement; it is now almost universally used for drains and vents and in many areas is accepted for hot as well as cold supply lines.

While remodeling in most rooms of the house can proceed at a leisurely pace, kitchens and bathrooms require relatively swift transitions to minimize the loss of their important functions. Have everything you need on hand before you begin. Do not rely on promised delivery dates of fixtures and supplies, which often must be ordered from the manufacturer—a process that can take months. Stock up on nails, screws, solder, paint and tools, including special tools, such as a basin wrench (page 90) or a pipe cutter (page 106), which may have to be borrowed or rented. And do not overlook replacement parts—the hacksaw blade always seems to break on a weekend after the hardware stores close.

When you are ready to begin, save time and effort by working in an area as uncluttered as possible. Remove furniture, appliances, fixtures, cabinets and carpeting wherever practical. Working around them, or removing them piecemeal, not only slows things down but exposes them to unnecessary damage. Place doormats at all entrances and hang sheets in open passageways to keep dust and debris out of the rest of the house; if you will be chipping dusty plaster, wet the sheets for additional protection.

Allot enough time to do the job thoroughly and without haste, and allow for delays. If you plan to have a professional handle tricky parts of the job—running a watertight vent up through a flat roof, for instance—be sure that your schedules are coordinated. Your own schedule, though, should be flexible enough to keep you going; do not place yourself in a position where everything comes to a standstill while you wait for a workman who arrives late or not at all.

The best way to minimize the temporary loss of a kitchen or bathroom during remodeling is to work midday or at night, between the peak-use periods of early morning and late afternoon. You may want to set up a temporary kitchen elsewhere in the house, and if you are doing extensive bathroom work in a home with children, it might be wise to establish protocol for use of a neighbor's facilities.

Clearing the Way for a Major Renovation

Removing old kitchen and bathroom fixtures to make room for new ones is mainly a task of loosening nuts and bolts. Most sinks, lavatories, toilets and bathtubs can be disconnected with such simple tools as a screwdriver and a variety of wrenches, including a basin wrench (below), used in cramped spaces.

Always begin by cutting off the water supply nearest the fixtures. Usually this involves closing valves on the fixture's supply lines. But for old fixtures that have no valves, you may have to shut down the entire house supply.

Examine old fixtures carefully to see how they are mounted and connected. You may have to use some of the techniques illustrated here and overleaf to remove them. Old sinks and lavatories may hang from a wall, rest on a pedestal or be suspended under a countertop. Faucet assemblies may extend down through holes in the fixture or they may not be attached at all, extending through holes in the wall or countertop. By comparison, removing a toilet (page 92) is usually easy—though sometimes messy. It takes only a few minutes to empty the tank and dismount a toilet. But because a toilet's trap is an integral part of the bowl, water will remain in it until the bowl is tilted—sometimes inadvertently —allowing the water to discharge.

Disconnecting a bathtub is greatly facilitated if there is an access panel to the pipes. Otherwise the plumbing will have to be disconnected from inside the tub by unscrewing the chrome strainer and overflow plate—which often have no exposed surface to which a wrench can be applied. In such cases you may have to improvise a tool (page 92).

Removing Sinks and Lavatories

1 **Disconnecting water supply lines.** Turn off the hot and cold supply valves. Unscrew the top coupling nuts, using a basin wrench (right) if space is too cramped for an adjustable wrench. If there are shutoff valves on the supply lines, also unscrew the coupling nuts above the valves to free the supply lines (inset). If there are no valves, remove the uncoupled supply lines after the sink or lavatory has been lifted off.

Once a bathtub is disconnected, it requires careful handling and some brawny helpers. In a small bathroom the toilet and lavatory may have to be taken out— even if you must later reinstall them—to provide enough space to maneuver the tub from its recess. Steel and fiberglass tubs can be lifted and carried out by two people. But a standard cast-iron tub weighs about 300 pounds and requires a team of four people to lift it. To remove such a tub you may have to open a wall (page 93)—or have the tub demolished by professionals.

In most cases, however, it is possible to salvage all or part of a removed fixture for use elsewhere. But keep in mind that fixtures are fragile and easily damaged when dropped or bumped; china toilets can crack, porcelain lavatories are likely to chip and steel sinks can be dented.

You can save parts of a fixture by removing them carefully and making a sketch of the parts before placing them in a container. But remember that a set of handsome faucets from an old lavatory is unlikely to fit a new one.

When fixtures have been removed, it is important to seal open supply lines and drain outlets immediately with caps or plugs of the identical material (page 93). This will keep sewer gas from seeping in through the drains, and will also protect the pipes from being clogged by construction debris until they are connected to the new fixtures. If a plumbing wall is to be broken through or torn down (pages 94-95), the pipes must be removed, rerouted or cut back to the floor before the openings are sealed.

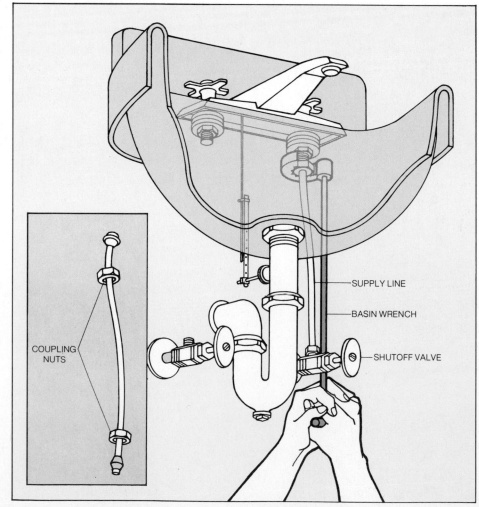

COUPLING NUTS

SUPPLY LINE

BASIN WRENCH

SHUTOFF VALVE

2 **Disconnecting the trap.** Place a bucket beneath the trap and unscrew the cleanout plug to drain it, then unscrew the slip nut to free the trap from the tailpiece *(right)* or garbage disposer. If there is a dishwasher, disconnect its drain hose by loosening the hose clamp *(page 123)*. If you are working on a lavatory, as shown here, you may have to disconnect the pop-up drain—by unscrewing the retainer nut—if the faucet assembly is fastened to a countertop *(below)*.

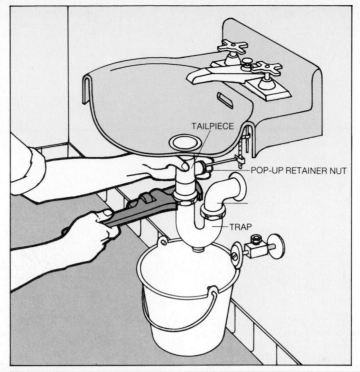

TAILPIECE

POP-UP RETAINER NUT

TRAP

3 **Dismounting a countertop installation.** Lay a 2-by-4 across the basin top and connect a wire from the 2-by-4 through the drain hole to a wood block. Twist the block until it rests against the tailpiece *(below)*. Unscrew the lug bolts *(inset)* and untwist the block to lower the basin.

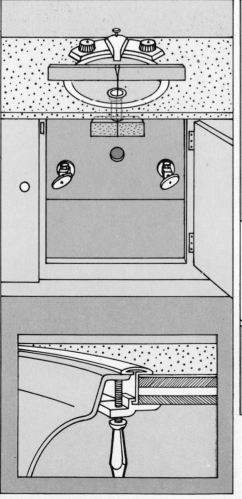

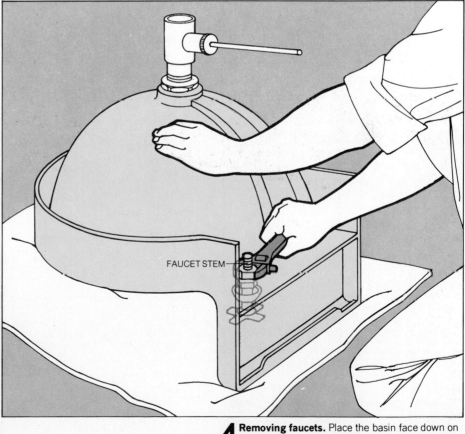

FAUCET STEM

4 **Removing faucets.** Place the basin face down on the floor—using padding if you intend to reuse it. Unscrew the lock nuts from the faucet stems and lift out the washers. Turn the basin face up and tap the faucets to break their seal of plumber's putty, then lift out the faucet assembly.

Taking Out a Toilet

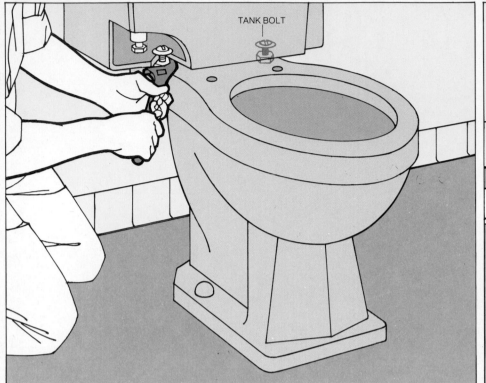

TANK BOLT

FLANGE BOLT

1 Disconnecting tank and bowl. Turn off the supply valve, flush the toilet, then bail and sponge the remaining water from the tank and bowl. Disconnect the supply line in the same way as a sink line (page 90). If the tank is mounted on the bowl, unscrew the nuts under the bowl's rear rim (above), using a helper, if necessary, to hold a screwdriver on the boltheads to keep them from turning. If the tank is mounted on the wall, remove the L-shaped spud pipe connecting it to the bowl by loosening the slip nuts at each end. Then remove the screws or bolts that hold the tank to the wall. Pry off the caps over the flange bolts and unscrew the nuts. Rock the bowl to break the putty seal with the flange, then lift it free.

2 Scraping the flange. Remove the flange bolts and scrape the gasket with a putty knife. Inspect the flange for cracks or wear and replace it if necessary. Stuff the hole with rags to prevent sewer gas from escaping.

Taking Out a Tub

1 Disconnecting the drains. Remove the access panel, if there is one. If there is no access panel, you can make one by cutting a 14-by-14-inch hole from floor level on the wall surface opposite the tub's head. But be careful not to damage the supply pipes. With pipes exposed, loosen the slip nut connecting the waste and overflow pipes to the drain outlet (right).

You can also disconnect the tub by removing the overflow plate (page 119), lift linkage and strainer. If there is no strainer screw, pry an old screwdriver under the edge to raise a dimple. Then place the screwdriver in the dimple and tap counterclockwise to free the strainer. With the strainer removed, insert pliers handles firmly into the crosspiece beneath. Use a pry bar to twist the crosspiece counterclockwise (inset), disconnecting waste and overflow pipes.

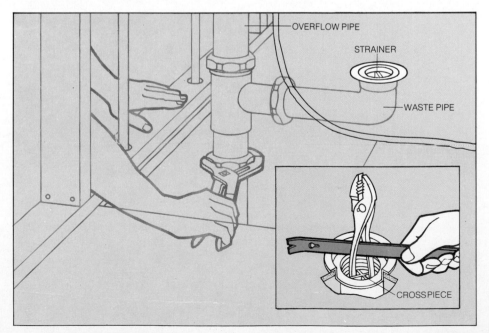

OVERFLOW PIPE

STRAINER

WASTE PIPE

CROSSPIECE

2 Freeing tub flanges. If there is a tile wall around the tub, use a cold chisel and hammer to chip away the tub molding and the first course of tile above the tub (*right*) to free the flange. If the wall is plaster, wallboard or laminate panels, cut away at least 4 inches above the tub. If the tub is steel or fiberglass, you must also remove screws or nails that hold the flange to the studs.

3 Removing the tub. Pry a steel or fiberglass tub away from the wall and have someone help you to carry it away—turning it on end if necessary to get it through doorways. You will need more help to pry loose and lift a cast-iron tub. And if the tub is enclosed by three walls, you may have to cut a hole through an end wall—preferably at the foot of the tub, where there are no supply pipes—at least 1 foot higher and wider than the tub. Lay down some heavy planks and push the tub out through the wall (*below*).

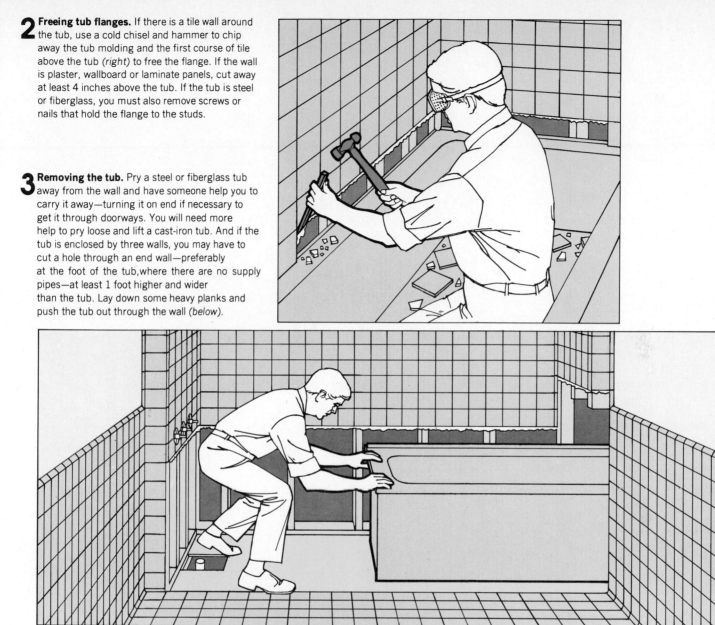

Capping Pipes

All pipes should be sealed when a fixture is removed. Supply lines with shutoff valves require only tape over the valve outlet hole. But drain outlets and supply lines without shutoff valves should be tightly capped. If the pipe is threaded, screw on a cap of the same material. Elbows and short pipe extenders, which have female threads, require plugs. For unthreaded plastic pipes, cement on a plastic cap; for unthreaded copper pipes, solder on a copper cap.

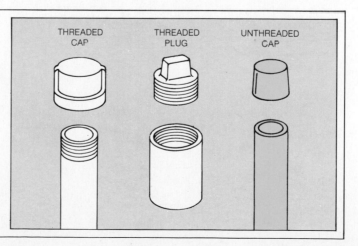

THREADED CAP THREADED PLUG UNTHREADED CAP

Tearing Down an Old Wall

To create space for a new bathroom or an expanded kitchen you can remove all or part of an interior wall—a job less formidable than it sounds. Most walls are nonbearing and can be quickly torn down without weakening the structure of your house, and you can usually avoid tearing down a bearing wall *(page 60)*. Only short wall spans need be removed to accommodate new bathrooms so more options are possible; a nonbearing wall can be chosen for removal. In enlarging a kitchen, a pass-through can open up space and allow passage of conversation and food, and cutting a pass-through *(pages 60-62)* is far easier than removing a bearing wall.

Before removing any wall or part of one, check that you can reroute or cut back pipes, air ducts and cables passing through the wall. You then begin by skinning the wall. Power tools often used to remove the surfaces of the wall cannot be used with the typical tile wall of a kitchen or bathroom. Instead, the tile and material under it are broken up with a heavy hammer and ripped free with gloved hands and pry bar *(Step 1)*. To save the tiles, though, pry them off before attacking the wall *(page 9)*. If your wall is wallboard, plaster or paneling, the job can be accomplished faster by using a circular saw, set to the depth of the wall covering, to saw out sections between the studs. But even with such a plain wall, some prefer hammer and hands to power tools to avoid the showers of dust the circular saw kicks up.

Demolishing the skeleton and patching the gaps is done the same way, whatever skinning method you choose. In any case, wear goggles at all times and don protective gloves when tearing away at the wall surface.

1 Tearing away the wall surface. Turn off the power to any circuits running to or through the wall to be demolished. Smash up the wallboard, or plaster and lath, between the studs on one side of the wall, using a heavy hammer. Wear protective gloves to rip the broken sections free. Use a pry bar to lever the stubborn bits of wallboard from the studs to which they are nailed. In a wall of plaster and metal lath, use your hammer to knock a small area of plaster from the lath about midway between two studs, then make a cut in the exposed metal lath with metal snips. Wearing gloves, rip along the cut to the stud. Continue breaking up the plaster and tearing the lath, finally prying any remaining pieces from the stud.

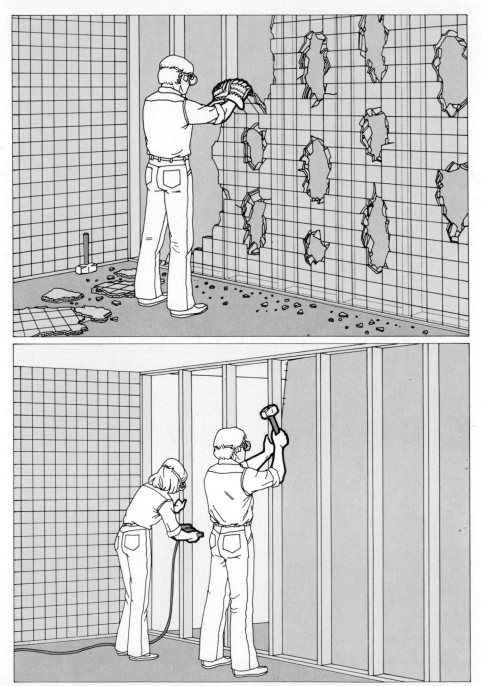

2 Removing the second wall surface. In the same room, hammer free the back of the plasterboard panels—or the strips of wood or metal lath supporting a plaster wall—along the length of the studs to which they are nailed. Then use your hands to push entire 4-by-8 wallboard panels free of the studs and into the adjoining room. With plaster walls, chunks will fall into the next room and you can then rip or pry the lath free from the studs. Cut all but the end studs in half and work the halves free from the sole and top plates.

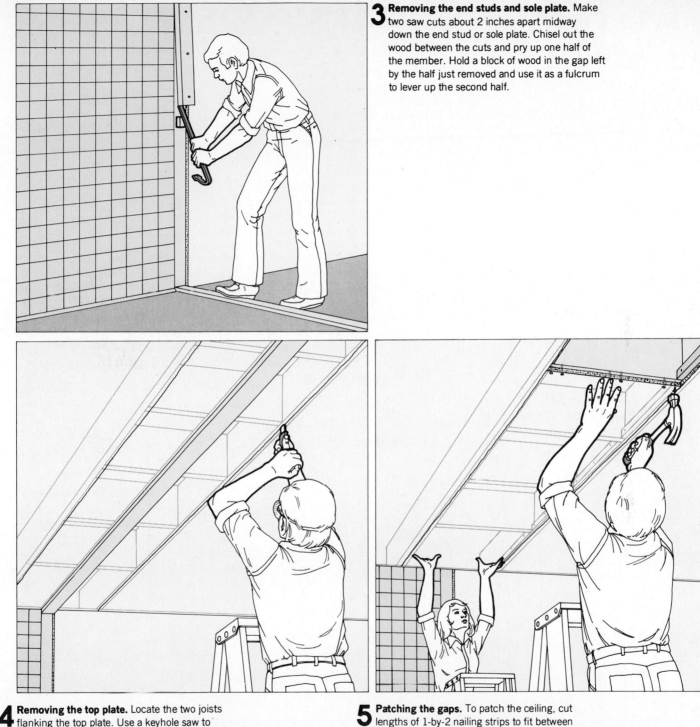

3 **Removing the end studs and sole plate.** Make two saw cuts about 2 inches apart midway down the end stud or sole plate. Chisel out the wood between the cuts and pry up one half of the member. Hold a block of wood in the gap left by the half just removed and use it as a fulcrum to lever up the second half.

4 **Removing the top plate.** Locate the two joists flanking the top plate. Use a keyhole saw to cut the ceiling along the inside edges of the joists. Stop when you reach a block of wood to which the top plate is attached and continue cutting on the other side of the block. Then use a utility knife to score the gaps in the ceiling cuts directly below the blocks. Use a hammer to break up the wallboard or plaster and wood lath between the ceiling cuts and tear away the broken sections with gloved hands. (Metal lath is rarely used behind plaster for a ceiling.) Pry the top plate loose from the blocks.

5 **Patching the gaps.** To patch the ceiling, cut lengths of 1-by-2 nailing strips to fit between the blocks along the two joists and nail them to the joists flush with the bottom edges. Cut sections of plasterboard to fit the ceiling opening and nail them to the nailing strips and blocks. Patch the cracks with perforated tape and joint compound. Nailing strips are not necessary for the gaps in the wall; anchor the wallboard directly to the blocks to which the end studs were attached. The floor gap can be filled with a piece of wood the same thickness as the floor and then covered with tile or other finish flooring.

How to Run Pipes through Walls and Floors

Building or rebuilding a kitchen or bathroom may involve the construction of walls—not just partitions, which are erected like those for any other part of a house, but the special kind called wet walls. A wet wall provides space for the plumbing pipes—particularly the big drain-waste-vent pipes—and is therefore thicker than an ordinary partition.

The easiest way to provide a new wet wall, if your plan and available space permit, is to add one to an existing wall. Just run the plumbing pipes along the surface of the old wall and attach them to the studs behind. Then nail furring strips to the wall and cover the pipes with a new wall surface (below).

When such a shortcut is not possible you then must erect a new wet wall. It is generally 6 inches thick, instead of the normal 4, and 2-by-6s are used for the horizontal sole and top plates. They may

also be used for the vertical studs, but the simpler construction shown here uses 2-by-4s set sideways and staggered so that there is space to thread pipes between studs, eliminating the need to drill holes.

The way the wet wall is installed will depend on the direction of the joists in the floor and ceiling of the room. If the new wall will run at right angles to the joists, nail the top and bottom plates of the frame to the edge of each ceiling and floor joist that they traverse. However, if the new wall will run parallel to the joists, position the frame under the most convenient ceiling joist, and nail the top plate to the joist through the ceiling. If you must locate the wall between joists, remove sections of the ceiling and install nailing blocks (opposite, top right).

Since a new wet wall is nonbearing, it supports little weight and the placement of studs is not crucial. Ordinarily they are

set at 24-inch intervals, but if the position of one interferes with the placement of a fixture, reposition it as necessary.

Although supply pipes can be run through ordinary 4-inch walls by cutting holes or notches in their framing, it is not advisable to install the large drain-waste-vent plumbing this way—the large cuts that are necessary will weaken the wall. For the same reason, avoid as far as possible running drains through joists, since they are always part of the basic house structure, and the large holes will weaken them, too. If you must saw or notch studs, joists or top plates, be sure to reinforce them as shown on page 103.

With your walls in place and the roughing-in dimensions marked, you can install the supporting members for your new fixtures. Finally, run the new pipes to the desired locations and install the fixtures themselves (pages 118-125).

An Easy Way to Make a Wet Wall

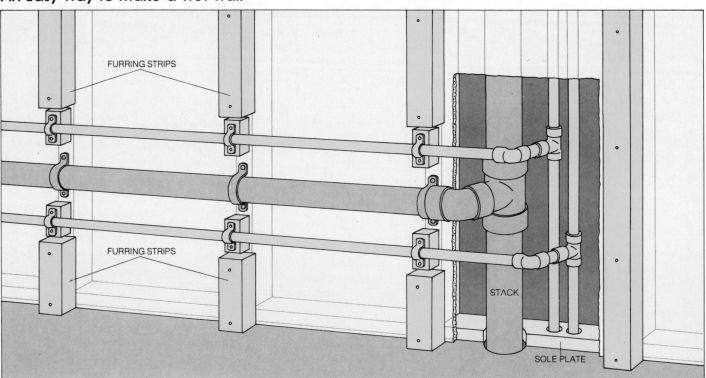

Furring out the wall. Cut out a section from the existing wall, up to 4 feet high, between the two studs where you plan to install the new stack. Cut a hole in the floor and the sole plate for the new stack and drill holes in the sole plate for the risers. Run the pipes through the holes and clamp the pipes to the studs. Cut strips of wood thick enough to project just beyond the pipes and nail these strips to the studs along the entire length of the wall. Make rough-in holes in new wallboard panels (pages 84-85), then nail the panels to the furring strips.

A New Wall Designed for Piping

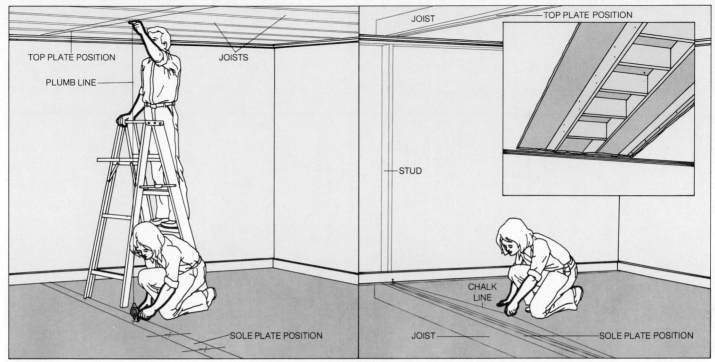

TOP PLATE POSITION

PLUMB LINE

JOISTS

SOLE PLATE POSITION

JOIST

STUD

TOP PLATE POSITION

CHALK LINE

JOIST

SOLE PLATE POSITION

1 **Locating the sole plate and top plate.** For new walls that run at right angles to the room joists, simply mark the position of the top plate on the ceiling and use a plumb line to find the corresponding spot on the floor for the sole plate (*above, left*). If the new wall runs parallel to the room joists, find the ceiling joist nearest the intended spot for the frame and position the sole plate and top plate so that the edge of the new wall frame overlaps the joist. Mark both positions with a chalk line (*above, right*).

If you must locate the wall between joists, cut away the ceiling to expose the two closest joists, then install a series of nailing blocks, of the same size lumber as the joists, at 24-inch intervals between the joists (*inset*). After installing the blocks, patch the strip with wallboard.

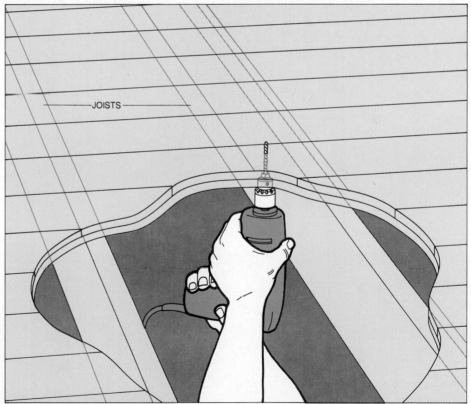

JOISTS

2 **Cutting a hole for the new stack.** If the floor joists run parallel to the new wet wall, drill a small locating hole from the room below for the stack. Make sure that the stack hole will clear the joist. On the floor of the room above, center the pipe on the hole, draw its outline and saw out the outlined area. When the floor joists run at right angles to the new wall, drill the locating hole from above. If you hit a joist, relocate the stack a few inches to either side of the hole. Drill two smaller holes for the supply pipes. Use an extension bit to drill through a finished ceiling.

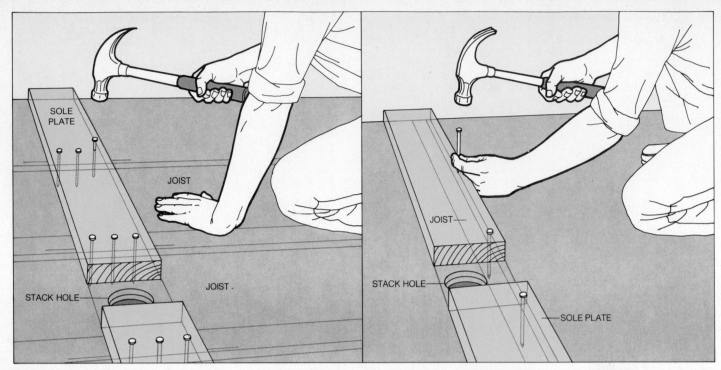

SOLE PLATE

JOIST

STACK HOLE

JOIST

JOIST

STACK HOLE

SOLE PLATE

3 **Installing the sole plate.** Remove the floor and
ceiling molding from the two walls the new wet
wall will touch. Cut two 2-by-6s the length of the
distance between the two walls. Use a 2-by-6
as the sole plate and lay it in place on the floor.
Mark the position of the hole for the vent stack
and cut the sole plate across its width about an
inch to each side of the hole. Reposition the
two parts of the sole plate and nail them to the
floor joists with 16-penny nails; drive three
nails at each joist (above, left). If the sole plate
runs parallel to floor joists, nail the sole plate
at 1-foot intervals, ¾ inch from the edge of the
sole plate (above, right).

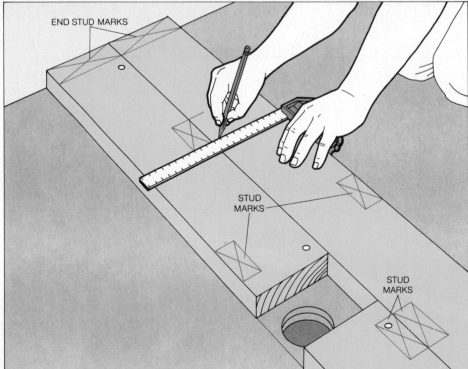

END STUD MARKS

STUD
MARKS

STUD
MARKS

4 **Marking the top plate and sole plate.** Mark positions for end studs at the ends of the sole
plate. Then along one edge of the sole plate, mark
positions at 24-inch intervals for one row of intervening studs. Along the other edge of the sole
plate, mark positions for a second row of
studs, each set midway between a pair in the first
row. Place the top plate beside the sole plate,
and with a carpenter's square, transfer the stud
marks from the sole plate to the top plate.

5 **Assembling the frame.** To determine the length of the studs, drop a plumb line from the ceiling to the floor at three points, and measure the height of the plumb line at each point; the three measurements should be within a fraction of an inch of one another. Take the minimum measurement (to make sure the frame will fit un- der the ceiling), subtract 3 inches for the com- bined thicknesses of the top and sole plates and cut to this length two 2-by-6 end studs and the necessary number of 2-by-4 studs. Nail the end studs in place through the top plates. Lay in- termediate studs on the floor, butt their ends to the top plate and nail them in place.

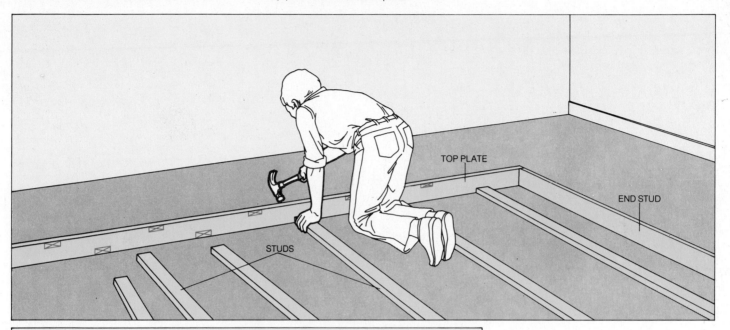

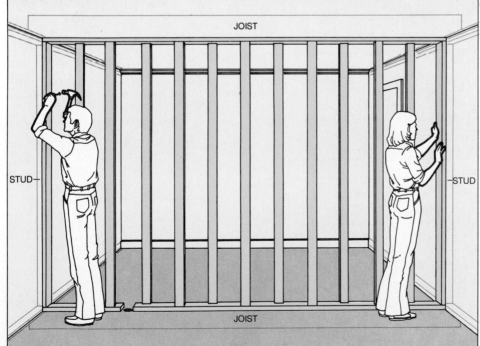

6 **Installing the wet-wall frame.** With a helper, lift the frame and place it on the sole plate so that the end studs rest on the sole-plate marks. Nail the top plate to a ceiling joist or joists, the same way you attached the sole plate to the floor *(opposite, top).* Nail the end studs to studs in the abutting walls. If the frame runs at right an- gles to the joists, do not nail the end studs to the walls unless you are certain that a stud stands directly behind each end stud. Toenail the end studs to the sole plate. Position each 2-by-4 stud at its mark on the sole plate. Use a level to check that the stud is vertical, shim it if necessary to make a snug fit then toenail it in place.

A Partition and a Prehung Door

An ordinary partition wall resembles the wet wall described on pages 96-99—with two important differences. The sole and top plates of a partition wall are 2-by-4s rather than 2-by-6s, and the studs are set across the plates rather than parallel to them. Like a wet wall, the partition is finished with wallboard.

Installing a door in such a wall is a simple matter of nailing a factory-made, prehung door to the sides and top of a doorway—technically, a rough doorframe—built into the partition. The doorway consists of two outer studs to which are nailed two jack studs; a horizontal crosspiece, called a header, tops the jack studs, and a short vertical stud, called a cripple stud, stands between the header and the top plate. The door assembly consists of two half jambs, pushed into the doorway from opposite sides of the wall; the halves join in a concealed tongue-and-groove joint. The door itself comes hinged to the inside of one jamb, with casing and doorstop attached.

Prehung doors are generally 6 feet 8 inches high, and 24, 30 or 32 inches wide. Buy the door assembly before you build the partition frame, and use its measurements as starting points for the built-in doorway. Cover the completed frame with wallboard to the edges of the doorway, then install the door assembly itself.

Many doors come with predrilled doorknob holes and bolt channels; to install a standard doorknob-bolt assembly, you need only drill a hole into the jamb for the bolt, and chisel mortises on the door and jamb for bolt and strike plates. Assemble the doorknobs and bolt in the door and screw the plates into place.

Building the wall and doorframes. Nail a 2-by-4 sole plate to the floor for the new wall and build a wall frame using 2-by-4 studs and top plate. Follow the method shown on pages 98-99, but set the studs across the plates and space them 24 inches apart to save lumber, local codes permitting; otherwise they must be 16 inches apart. Omit the studs that would stand in the doorway.

For the rough doorframe, install two ordinary studs as the outer studs, and space them 3½ inches farther apart than the width of the top jamb of the door assembly. Cut two jack studs 1¼ inches shorter than the top of the top jamb and nail them to the outer studs, and flush with the bottoms of the studs. Nail a 2-by-4 header between the outer studs and across the tops of the jack studs, and nail two 2-by-4 cripple studs between the header and the top plate. Install the wall frame on the sole plate (page 99, Step 6) and complete the doorframe by cutting away the part of the sole plate lying between the jack studs.

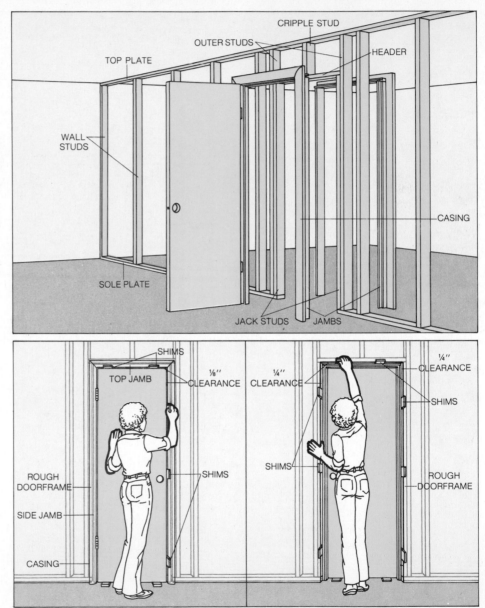

Installing the door. Remove the shipping braces holding the half jambs together and slide the half jamb containing the door into the doorframe. Support the door on scraps of wood and insert three ⅛-inch shims between the strike side of the door and the jamb, and two between the top of the door and the top jamb (above, left). Nail the casing to the frame. From the other side of the wall, insert two ¼-inch shims between the top jamb and the frame, and three shims between each side jamb and the rough frame (above, right); break the shims off at the edge of the jambs and fasten the jambs to the frame with nails driven through the shims. Slide the other half jamb into position—it must fit snugly to the other half jamb—and nail the casing to the wall. Nail the jamb to the frame at 1-foot intervals and remove the shims wedging the door closed.

Supporting Pipe and Fixtures

Each of the basic bathroom fixtures—toilet, lavatory and bathtub—requires special supports, adapted to the type and location of the fixture. You need some of the same supports in a powder room. In a kitchen you would probably install a countertop support for the sink.

The toilet is usually the closest fixture to the drain-waste-vent stack. The toilet waste pipe curves sharply under the toilet at a section called the closet bend; because of the pressure of the water and wastes rushing through the closet bend, it must have especially strong support. If the toilet waste pipe crosses a joist, cut away a short span of the joist and frame the cut section for support (right).

Special supports for a bathroom lavatory are less common—most lavatories are set into a countertop—but some models hang from a homemade crosspiece set into the wall (right, bottom).

The bathtub, largest of the fixtures, is in some ways the easiest to support (page 102), but you must also cut an access hole in the floor for the tub drain and the overflow pipe, and install crosspieces in the wall to support the faucet and shower assemblies. If the drain-and-overflow assembly lies over a joist, and the tub cannot be repositioned, cut the joist and frame the cut section for support.

With all the supports in place, you can run the drainpipes and supply pipes, supported along their routes (page 103) to the fixture locations. If you run pipe through notches or holes in studs, top plates or joists, be sure to reinforce the cuts (page 103). Joists may present a special problem. The pitch of a long section of drain-waste pipe may force you to hang pipe below the joists; if you wish, hide the pipes with a dropped ceiling.

A bathtub calls for one final job of carpentry—not for support, but to give easy access to the trap for emergency repairs. When you have installed all the fixtures and put up the wall surfaces (box, page 103, bottom), move to the adjoining room and cut a square opening between two studs in the wall directly behind the tub and at floor level. Screw a piece of plywood the same thickness as the wallboard onto the opening.

A Brace for a Closet Bend

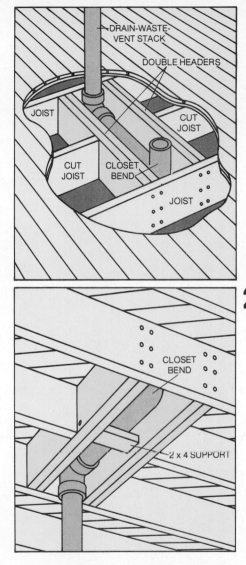

1 **Reinforcing a cut joist.** Determine the direction of the floor joists. If the toilet waste pipe to the stack will run parallel to the joists, install the pipe between two joists (pages 104-107)—if necessary, cut out a ceiling section below to make the installation—and proceed to Step 2. If the waste pipe will run across the joists and you cannot suspend the pipe below the joists, you must cut the intervening joist. Make the cut from the room below; if the room is finished, remove a ceiling section about 18 inches wide, exposing the joist you must cut and extending to the two on either side. Cut the exposed joist along the edges of this opening, and cut four headers to fit between the uncut joists. Nail two headers to each cut joist and to the uncut joists. Install the closet bend (pages 104-107).

2 **Installing the support.** Cut a 2-by-4 support to fit between joists or headers. Set the support under the waste pipe, about midway between the closet bend and the stack, with the wide side of the support against the pipe; nail the support to the joists or the headers.

A Bracket for a Lavatory

Installing a crosspiece and brackets. Cut a 2-by-4 crosspiece 3 inches longer than the distance between studs. Hold the piece across the two studs at the lavatory position, with each end of the crosspiece overlapping a stud by 1½ inches; check the horizontal alignment of the piece with a carpenter's level, then mark the top and bottom of the piece on the studs. With a hammer and chisel, notch the studs within the marks, wedge the crosspiece into the notches with the front of the piece flush to the fronts of the studs, and nail the piece in place. Cover the wall with wallboard and screw the bracket to the crosspiece through the wall surface.

Framing for a Bathtub

1 Cutting a hole for the drain and overflow. Cut a hole in the floor about 1 foot square, centered on the rough-in mark for the drain hole and extending to the sole plate. If the opening lies over a joist and you cannot shift the position of the tub, cut out a section of the joist along the edges of the opening. Cut four headers to fit between the uncut joists and nail two headers to the end of each cut joist and to the uncut joists.

2 Installing shower and faucet supports. Rough-in dimensions (*page 85*) indicate the vertical heights of the faucet assembly and the shower head and their horizontal distance behind the wall. At the indicated heights of the assembly and the head, mark the end stud and the front or back stud that lies closest to the horizontal position. Nail a 1-by-2 or 2-by-4 horizontal support at each pair of marks. The supports must lie at the correct distance behind the wall: use a block of wood to set this distance on the end stud and, if necessary, nail blocks of wood to the front stud (*near right*) or the back stud (*far right*) to bring the supports into position. Screw the faucet assembly and shower head to the supports.

3 Supporting the tub. Cut three 2-by-4 tub flange supports to the exact height specified in rough-in dimensions. Nail the supports to the studs that lie nearest the ends and center of the tub. Minor height corrections can be made by shimming after the tub is installed (*page 118*).

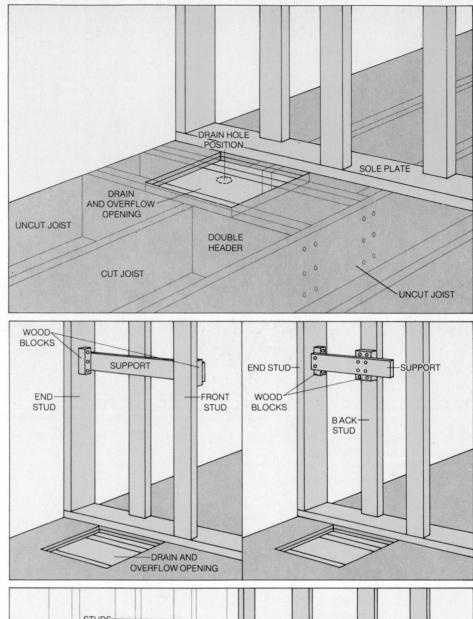

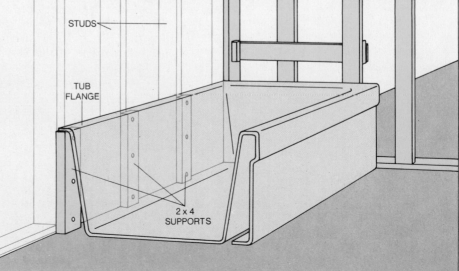

Safe Passages for Pipes

In a wet wall. Run new pipe between the back and front studs of a wet wall, clamping the pipe to either row of studs. Use clamps designed for the type of pipe you are using and secure the pipe to each stud along its path.

In studs. Run pipe through notches up to 2½ inches square or through holes within 1½ inches of stud edges. Reinforce a notch with a ⅛-inch steel plate mortised into the stud; in a bearing wall, add a stud at right angles to it.

In top plates. Cut a hole for a stack through the center of the top plates. To reinforce the hole, cut two 2-by-4 supports and notch them at their centers to fit around the pipe. Nail the supports to the top of the plates.

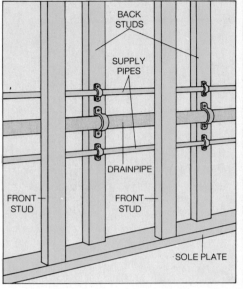

In joists. Notches and holes make passages for pipe in joists as well as studs, but must be more strongly reinforced. Cut a joist notch to no more than one quarter of the joist's height, and locate it in one of the outer quarters of the joist's length; reinforce the notch with a 2-by-4 nailed to both sides of the joist directly under the notch. The maximum safe diameter of a joist hole is one quarter of the joist's height, at a location at least 2 inches from the top and bottom edges. Caution: Limit runs of drain and waste pipe through holes to short distances—on a long run, the pitch of the pipe will locate one or more holes too close to the edges of the joists.

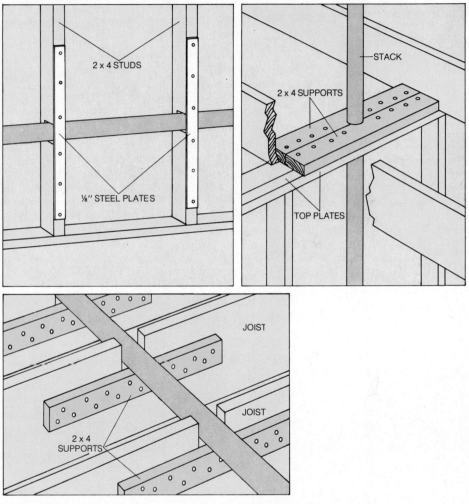

Special Wallboard for a Damp Room

Wallboard for such high-moisture areas as bathrooms and kitchens goes into place as easily as in any other room of the house—but it is no ordinary wallboard. The type used in other rooms absorbs moisture through its paper cover, and in a damp room its core becomes soft and spongy. The wallboard designed for bathrooms and kitchens has a tough, almost waterproof cover, and its core is saturated with asphalt to resist absorption and softening.

Water-resistant wallboard is scored, snapped and cut in exactly the same way as the standard type. Before putting it up, rough-out all the plumbing in the room, and cut holes in the wallboard to accommodate the protruding pipes. Then nail the new wallboard into place.

A sheet of water-resistant wallboard 4 by 8 feet weighs about 10 pounds more than a sheet of standard wallboard, and calls for a different nailing arrangement: you must space nails at 6-inch intervals, rather than 1 foot apart as for standard wallboard, and be sure that the greater weight is adequately supported. Water-resistant wallboard is best supported on studs 16 inches on center. If the studs on your wall are farther apart, or if you plan to cover the wall with tiles more than ⁵⁄₁₆ inch thick, add a horizontal 2-by-4 support between the centers of each pair of studs, and nail the wallboard to the supports as well as to the studs themselves.

Getting Rid of Wastes: The Drain System

A trouble-free drain installation takes careful planning and execution. In a limited space, you must accommodate drainpipes for all the fixtures you are putting in, slope these pipes downward toward a main drain called a stack, and vent the stack to the outdoors *(page 108)*. You must clear your plans for this entire drain-waste-vent (DWV) system with a local plumbing inspector—drains are the most strictly regulated area of plumbing—and the system must be tested to pass inspection *(page 111)*.

The job has been made easier for amateur plumbers by plastic pipe and fittings. Most plumbing codes now accept plastic as a material for drain systems (if yours does not, use copper, following the methods shown on pages 112-113). Plastic pipe is lightweight, durable and easily joined with solvent cement. It can be cut with a hacksaw, but you must make straight cuts at right angles to the pipe; to be sure of your cuts, you may prefer a backsaw and miter box or a pipe cutter specially made for plastic DWV pipe.

Because DWV pipe and fittings must carry the flow of wastes by gravity alone, the interior of a completed installation is a smooth continuous surface. For example, a DWV T—called a sanitary T—has a branch inlet that curves into the pipe run rather than joining it at a right angle; it must be installed so that the branch curves into the flow, not against it. A drainpipe must slope downward, either at a sharp angle of 45° or more, or, in a horizontal run, at a pitch of about ¼ inch for each foot of the run (avoid a pitch of less than ⅛ inch or more than ½ inch—the pipe is likely to clog).

A complete drain run begins with a trap—a U-shaped section of pipe in which water collects to block the passage of sewer gases into living areas. Toilets have built-in traps; the trap for a lavatory is usually a separate assembly, installed with the fixture *(page 118)*; a shower or tub trap is part of the drain system, installed below the floor.

Beyond the trap, a shower or tub drain may feed into an inlet in the side of a closet bend—a large, gently curved elbow that receives waste from the toilet.

In turn, the closet bend feeds into a large sanitary T through a straight section of pipe. This closet-bend and sanitary-T assembly is the heart of the new drain system: when the shower, tub or lavatory drain is not connected to the closet bend, it usually connects to an inlet in the side of the sanitary T. Other inlets in the sanitary T can handle wastes from such fixtures as a lavatory or a bidet.

When choosing and routing the pipes of the system, follow simple rules and practices. If your code permits, choose 3-inch pipe for the main part of the run and the toilet drain; 1½- or 2-inch pipe, depending on the venting arrangement *(page 108)*, for branch drains to showers, tubs and lavatories. Use elbows in the waste line to avoid obstacles; with a series of elbows you can, if necessary, run the line completely around the walls of a basement. For a second-story bath, remove part of the floor and the ceiling below; run the waste stack up from the basement next to the wall of the room below, then conceal the pipe in a wallboard enclosure.

From Closet Bend to Soil Branch

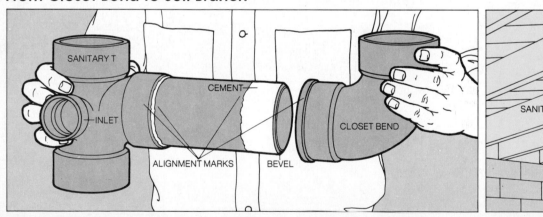

1 Joining a closet bend and a sanitary T. Cut a hole in the flooring between two joists for a drain stack *(page 98)*. Using the rough-in dimensions *(pages 84-85)* supplied by the toilet manufacturer, locate and cut a hole in the floor for the toilet drain. Cut and test-fit a length of pipe to connect a closet bend and a sanitary T; the pipe should be exactly long enough to center the closet bend under the toilet drain hole and the sanitary T under the stack hole. (If you plan to drain a lavatory or shower through the sanitary T or closet bend, be sure that the inlet points toward the fixture location.) Make alignment marks where the fittings meet the pipe, so that you can realign the joints quickly after applying cement. With a jackknife or a file, remove any burrs from inside the pipe ends and bevel the outside edges of the ends slightly. Working quickly, apply a thin layer of cement to the inside end of each fitting and a thick layer to the outside end of the pipe. Press and twist the parts together, matching up the alignment marks. An unbroken bead of cement should be visible all the way around the joint. If the bead is broken, separate the parts and apply more cement.

2 Installing the assembly. At the tops of the sanitary T and the closet bend, insert, but do not cement, lengths of pipe long enough to reach from the planned position of the closet-bend assembly to a point above the floor. Guide the pipes up through the holes in the floor and position the assembly, using a level to be sure that the sanitary T is exactly vertical. Nail a 1-by-2 support between joists and beneath the assembly; if the assembly lies below the joist level, hang it from a 1-by-2 support with a perforated iron strap. Jam thin wood wedges between the pipes and the openings in the floor.

3 Running pipe to the existing stack. Test-join an elbow to the bottom of the sanitary T with a short length of pipe. To one side of the planned path of the new soil branch, nail a strip of perforated iron strap to a joist or a 2-by-4 installed between joists; position the strip less than one pipe length from the elbow. On the other side of the branch path, drive a nail halfway in; be sure it has a head smaller than the strap holes. Fit a length of pipe into the elbow, and suspend it by looping the strap under the pipe and hooking the strap to the second nail. Hang the strap by different holes until the pipe slopes ¼ inch per foot; to check the slope, you can use a level with a strip of wood taped to one end to make the level read true at the correct pitch (a level 2 feet long will need a strip of wood ½ inch thick). Couple additional lengths of pipe to the first, adding an expansion joint every 20 feet, until you reach the existing soil stack. Add more straps to support the run at intervals of about 3 feet.

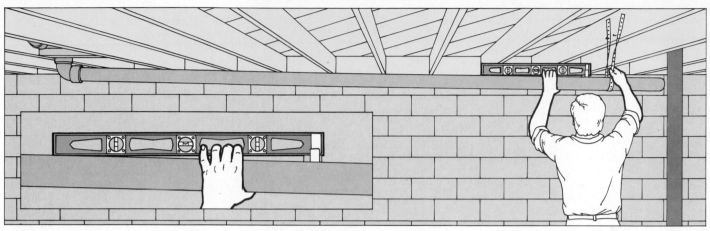

From Branch to Stack: At a Cleanout Plug

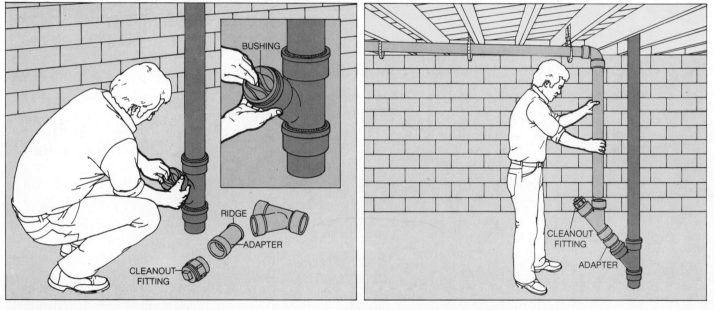

1 Adapting the cleanout. Unscrew the cleanout plug and replace it with a threaded plastic adapter; use a galvanized steel bushing if the threaded end of the adapter is too small. If you cannot find an adapter to fit, chisel out the lead and oakum from the joint between the stack and the insert that the cleanout plug fits into; remove the insert. Fit a rubber bushing into the stack by turning it halfway inside out and inserting it as shown above. Obtain a plastic-to-cast-iron adapter and saw off the end ridge. Insert the adapter into the rubber bushing. Join a Y to the adapter with a short piece of pipe. Position the Y with one end pointing upward, and cement a cleanout fitting into the slanted end.

2 Connecting the soil branch. Cut the end of the new branch at a point where the outlet of a quarter bend at the end run will be directly above the vertical inlet of the Y. Test-install the quarter bend and, by lifting the horizontal run in the straps, join it to the cleanout Y with pipe. Be careful not to alter the slope of the horizontal run.

Mark all the joints, disassemble the parts, then cement them together, beginning at the sanitary T, held stationary by a helper. At the straps along the horizontal run, replace the small-headed nails with large-headed ones. Cement a test cap (page 111) to the end of the last length of pipe just before the cleanout adapter.

From Branch to Stack: At a T

1 Bracing the stack. To keep a stack from dropping when cut *(Step 2)*, you must brace it where it enters the first floor. Find the point where the stack emerges from the basement. If it is behind a wall, drill a hole in the wall and probe for studs with a wire, then remove a 16-by-10-inch rectangle of wallboard between studs at floor level to reveal the stack. Set a stack clamp around the stack *(inset)*, about ½ inch above the sole plate or the floor; tighten the clamp bolts hard to grip the stack firmly. Drive wedges underneath the clamp, so that the sole plate or floor supports the weight of the stack. Fasten 2-by-4 nailing blocks to the sides of the studs and nail the wallboard back in place; patch the seams around the rectangle and repaint the wall.

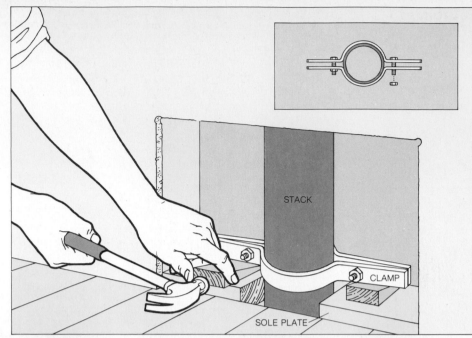

STACK

CLAMP

SOLE PLATE

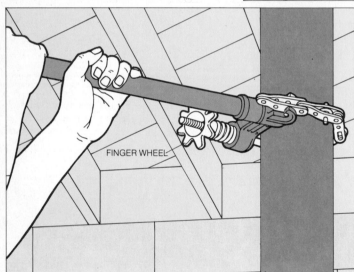

FINGER WHEEL

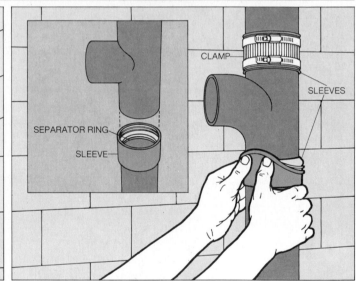

CLAMP

SLEEVES

SEPARATOR RING

SLEEVE

2 Opening the stack. Hold a hubless sanitary T, chosen to fit the existing stack and the new soil branch, against the stack at the proper height to receive the soil branch and mark the positions of the top and bottom of the T on the stack.

If you have a copper or plastic stack, it can be cut with a hacksaw. If you have to cut a cast-iron stack, a pipe cutter like the one shown above can be rented from most suppliers. Bring the cutting chain around the stack and slip it into the hooks on the other side of the tool head. Set the chain ¼ inch above the top mark on the stack, tighten the finger wheel to compress the spring, and move the handle of the cutter back and forth until the pipe separates. Make a second cut ¼ inch lower than the bottom mark, remove the section of pipe and stuff toilet tissue loosely into both of the cut ends of the stack.

3 Installing the T. Slide the stainless-steel ring of a pipe clamp onto the bottom of the cut stack. Fit the neoprene sleeve of the clamp over the pipe with the separator ridge inside the sleeve resting against the end of the pipe *(inset)*. Roll the sleeve on the bottom part of the stack back upon itself until the upper half is folded over the lower half. Repeat the process on the top part of the stack, folding the free end of the sleeve up. Place the sanitary T between the rolled sleeves, fold the sleeves over the ends of the T, then slide the stainless-steel rings over the sleeves and tighten the screws.

Cement the parts of the soil branch. Cut the end of the new soil branch to fit the end of the T and cement a test cap to the end of the pipe *(page 111)*. When you have tested the system, join the plastic pipe to the T with a pipe clamp.

A Drain for a Tub or Shower

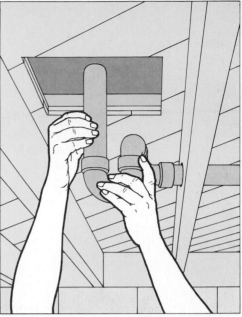

1 **Running the drain.** If space permits, the tub or shower drain should be run to the closet-bend assembly below the joists, supported by iron strap at a pitch of ¼ inch per foot *(page 105)*. Otherwise, run the drainpipe through holes in the joists *(page 103)*, setting the holes progressively lower as the pipe approaches the closet-bend assembly. At the assembly, the pipe may be connected to an inlet *(above)* or, if you are installing the vent shown in

the center of page 109, to an inlet in the closet bend. Many codes stipulate that a 1½-inch pipe without separate venting may be no longer than 4½ feet; a 2-inch pipe may run 5 feet. For longer drains that are individually vented, substitute a T for a coupling within these critical distances, as shown on page 109, top and center. To install pipe in joist holes, cut it into pieces that will fit between the joists, insert the pieces into the holes and join them with couplings.

2 **Installing the trap.** Trim the horizontal drainpipe to place the inlet of the trap directly beneath the rough-in center of the drain *(pages 84-85)*, adding an elbow, if necessary. Cement a piece of pipe to the trap inlet, long enough to extend above the floor when the trap is in place. If the trap comes in two pieces, cement the parts together. Test-fit the trap to the end of the pipe, mark the joint and cement the trap to the pipe.

Drains for a Toilet and a Lavatory

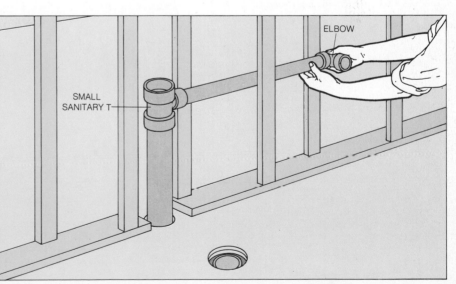

Extending a closet bend. To extend the inlet of the closet bend up to the proper height to receive the toilet flange *(page 120, Step 2)*, cut a length of pipe that will reach a point level with or slightly below the subfloor. With a helper bracing the closet bend from below, cement the pipe in the bend.

Connecting the lavatory drain. For a lavatory draining directly into the stack (an alternate drainage route is shown on page 109, center), remove the pipe from the top of the sanitary T. Cut a length of pipe to join this T to a smaller sanitary T at the level required by the rough-in specifications for the lavatory drain. With a helper

bracing the large T from below, cement the pipe into place. Test-fit, mark and cement the small T on top of the pipe. Run pipe inside the wall *(page 103)* from the inlet of the small T to the point where the drain will enter the wall; at the end of the pipe, install an elbow to accept the drain. Cement the parts together.

Letting the Drains Breathe

In every drain stack, a vertical section rises through the roof of the house to the air outside. Called the stack vent, it is crucial to a drain system. It releases noxious gases outside the house, and admits outside air to maintain atmospheric pressure in the drain system *(page 78)*. To make the venting part of the system work, a vent line runs from every fixture trap to a main stack. The trap-to-vent connection can be made in two different ways: by stack-, or self-venting, in which the fixture drainpipe both drains and vents the trap; and by individual, or branch-venting, in which a separate vent line links a trap (or, under some codes, a pair of traps) directly to the stack vent.

Stack-venting, the simpler of the two methods, is practical where a cluster of fixtures lies close to a drain stack—but it falls under especially tight code requirements. The pipe connecting the fixture to the stack must have a pitch of ¼ inch per foot, and must be shorter than the "critical distance" specified by your local code—typically, 4½ feet for 1½-inch pipe, 5 feet for 2-inch pipe and 6 feet for 3-inch pipe. The stack must not drain fixtures on a floor above, and under most codes a tub or shower must drain into the T of the closet-bend assembly.

If your plumbing plan does not meet these criteria, use the individual venting system, more complex in installation but flexible enough to accommodate almost any placement of your fixtures. An individual vent line must tap the pipe leading from the fixture trap at a point less than the critical distance from the trap; if this pipe turns sharply downward within the critical distance, the vent tap must leave the pipe before the turn. From the tap, the vent line must rise at an angle of no less than 45° to a level at least 6 inches higher than the flood rim of the fixture— that is, the level at which water would flow over the top of the fixture and onto the floor. If fixtures on a floor above drain into the stack, the vent line must rise above the level of the drain lines upstairs. The final connection to the vent stack is made by a nearly horizontal line, pitched slightly upward to prevent water from collecting in the pipe.

A new drain system can be vented to the outside of the house in two ways: It can rejoin the existing stack in the attic, or it can be taken through a hole cut in the roof *(pages 109-110)*. The pipe that runs through the roof must have a minimum diameter specified by your local code; if the vent stack in the house is smaller than this minimum, use an adapter to increase its size before it goes through the roof. Your plumbing code will also specify minimum clearances between the roof vent and the nearest windows, skylights or ventilation grilles.

A Stack for Self-venting

From the drain to the attic. Drop a plumb line from the top plate of the wet wall into the center of the lavatory T *(page 107)* and mark the position of the string on the plate. Cut a hole in the plate slightly larger than the vent pipe. If the attic is floored, use an extension bit held inside the opening in the top plate to drill a locator hole through the underside of the attic flooring. Find the hole in the attic and use it as a guide to cut a hole in the floor for the vent.

Cut a length of pipe long enough to reach from the T to a point about a foot into the attic; angle the pipe into the hole and cement it to the T.

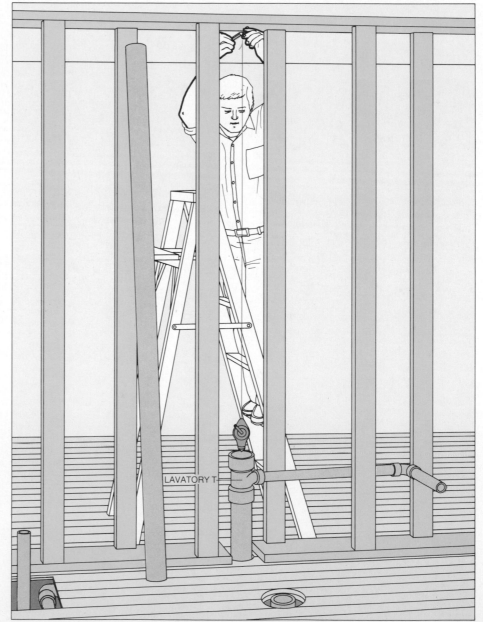

LAVATORY T

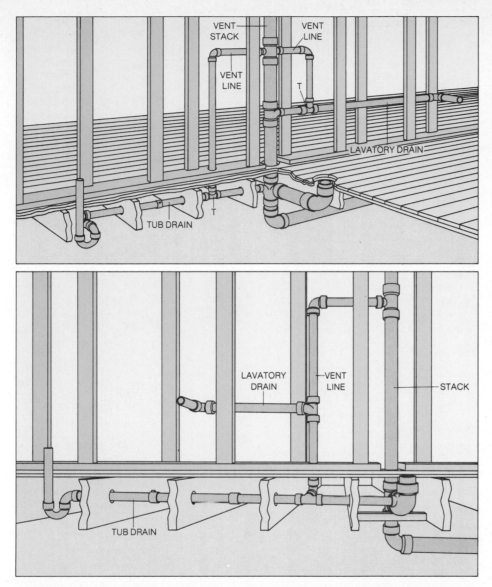

An Individual-Vent System

Completely separate vent lines. Starting at the stack *(center of picture)*, install the lavatory drain as on page 107 (extending to the right here) but include a T in the drain branch within the critical distance from the position of the lavatory trap. Extend the stack at least 6 inches above the lavatory flood rim, and install a cross fitting in the stack to receive vent lines from both the lavatory and the shower or tub. From a T installed in the shower or tub drain line (extending left from the stack here), route a vent pipe up through the sole plate and over to the cross fitting on the stack. With pipe and fittings, join the T in the lavatory drain line to the cross fitting.

A simplified vent line for two fixtures. If your local plumbing code permits you to vent two traps with a single line, you may be able to simplify the pattern of pipe as shown at left, although in some localities you must then use 2-inch pipe instead of the 1½-inch pipe generally acceptable for the tub and lavatory. As before, extend the stack upward from the top of the sanitary T to a point at least 6 inches above the flood rim of the lavatory *(right side of picture)*. Run pipe from a T in the shower or tub drain up through the sole plate to the level of the lavatory drain line. Install a T for the lavatory drain, and complete the vent with a line up from this T and over to a T installed in the stack. Connect the lavatory drain line to the lavatory drain T.

A Shortcut to Outside Air

A connection in the attic. Extend the stack up through the ceiling plate, into the attic and over to the existing stack. Install a T in the existing stack *(page 106)*, making the top cut in the stack first. The upper section of the stack may come loose at the roof as you work; if it does, have a helper hold it in place while you install the T. Join the vent line to the T. On the roof reseal the stack with roofing cement if necessary.

Going Outside through the Roof

1 **Cutting the hole.** In the attic, drop a plumb from the roof to the center of the stack vent, mark the position of the string on the underside of the roof and drive a nail through the mark. (If the stack rises directly under a rafter, alter its course with two 45° elbows to bring it to the roof between two rafters.) On the roof, find the nail and, using a saber or keyhole saw, cut a hole for the stack with the nail as a center.

2 **Installing the pipe.** To waterproof the exit hole of the stack, use a flashing plate with a precut hole and a rubber collar. Lubricate the collar with petroleum jelly and slip the top edge of the flashing up under the shingles above the stack hole until the flashing and stack holes match. (If any shingle nails get in the way, remove them with a pry bar.) Cut a length of stack pipe to reach the distance above the roof specified by your code. Have a helper angle the pipe up through the hole in the flashing while you hold the flashing in place on the outside of the roof.

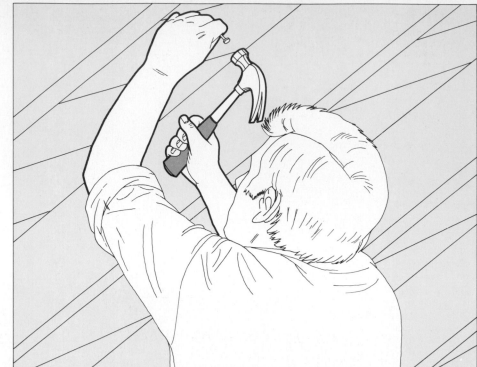

3 **Securing the flashing.** Lift the shingles that cover the top edge of the flashing and nail the flashing down with two roofing nails. Caulk around the flashing with roofing cement. On roll roofing, caulk the bottom of the flashing with roofing cement and press the flashing into place; then nail the flashing down and apply cement to the nailheads and around the edge of the flashing.

Testing All the Drains at Once

As the final step in installing a new drain system, you must test your work by filling the system with water and checking for leaks. When you have tested the system and repaired any leaks, you can call upon a plumbing inspector to give your work official approval.

Some codes require a second test after the fixtures are installed *(pages 118-125),* in which dense smoke or oil of peppermint is introduced into the system and leaks are spotted by sight or odor. This test is not strictly a part of the drain system installation: Its main purpose is to check the toilet drain seals.

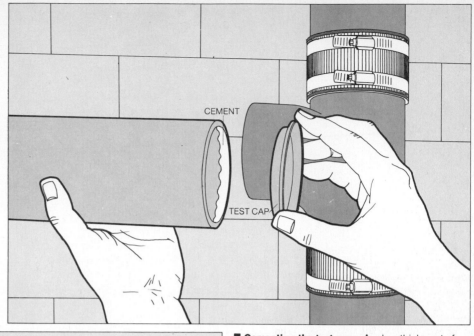

1 Cementing the test caps. Apply a thick coat of cement to the inside of each open pipe and press a test cap into place with a twisting motion. To remove the cap after the test, break it open with a hammer and pry the remaining fragments free with a screwdriver.

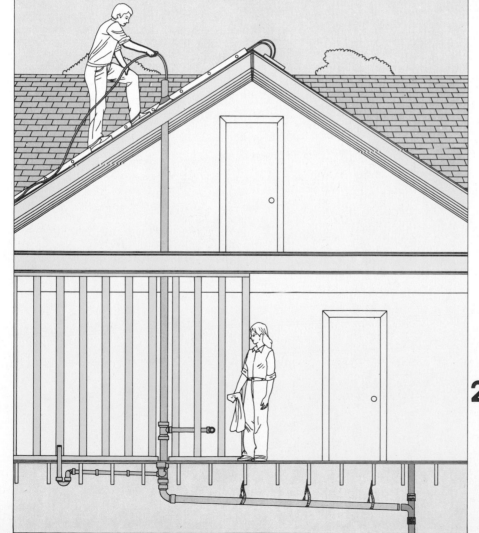

2 Checking for leaks. After blocking all openings with test caps, pour water into the stack vent on the roof to fill the drain system completely. If you find a leak, punch a small hole in the bottom test cap with an awl or ice pick and drain the water into a tub; let the system dry out overnight, then apply cement to the leaking joint. Plug the hole you made in the bottom test cap and re-test the system. If the leak persists, cut out the joint, replace the fitting and rejoin the pipe with couplings. Do not remove test caps until you are ready to connect the fixtures.

111

Getting Water to the Fixtures: The Supply System

Supplying a bathroom with hot and cold water is much easier than running pipes for wastes and drains. The supply lines need not be pitched, because the water in them is under pressure and will move in any direction; with Ts, elbows and angled fittings, you can run them around corners, ducts and other obstacles. If you can, avoid what plumbers call trapping the line—that is, running the pipes in a U shape that can trap water when you drain the system for repairs or for winter months when a summer place is empty. If a trapped line is unavoidable, install an outlet to empty the U *(opposite, top)*.

Local plumbing codes dictate the material of the pipe you use. Choose plastic if the code permits, and make cemented connections as shown on page 104. Otherwise, use copper tubing, almost as easy to install, and one of the most durable of all pipes. If your system consists of another metal, you can add new copper or plastic lines with transition fittings.

Along with the material you use, the code will also dictate pipe sizes. The size of a branch supply line is determined by the number of fixtures attached to it.

Most codes require ½-inch pipe for two fixtures, ¾ inch for more. In the system shown here, the cold-water line begins with ¾-inch tubing because it feeds three fixtures—a toilet, a lavatory and a tub. The hot-water line is ½ inch; it supplies only a lavatory and a tub.

Run hot and cold lines parallel to each other and at least 6 inches apart, and fasten them to studs or joists every 6 to 8 feet with copper pipe clamps. Choose the shortest, straightest route from existing hot- and cold-water lines to the new installation. You must, however, observe one basic rule: Never tap into a line smaller than the new branch lines.

With your route chosen, locate the shutoff valves that control the mains you will be cutting. Close the valves, and open all the faucets and flush all the toilets on the branch. If you tap a branch that does not have a shutoff valve, drain the entire house system: Close the main supply valve; then, starting at the top of the house, open all faucets and flush all toilets, and finally, open the drain faucet on the main supply line.

Before soldering a new fitting to a cut

copper pipe, poke a rag into the opened end to dry it out. If moisture remains in the line and prevents you from soldering, stuff a bit of stale bread into the wet pipe to absorb the moisture while you solder; the bread will disintegrate and flow out of the pipes through the taps when you restore the house water supply.

Elsewhere, be sure to take safety precautions when you solder pipe near a wall or ceiling. Protect these surfaces with an asbestos sheet (some plumbers also wet exposed areas before they begin to solder). You can reduce the amount of soldering you do in flammable areas by test-fitting sections to be sure you have measured correctly and then soldering the sections at a workbench. Wear safety glasses when soldering overhead.

When you have completed an installation, test the new lines for leaks. Cap the ends of the lines *(page 93)*, then open the shutoff valves in the new supply branches and fill the lines with water. Wait at least 24 hours before concealing the pipes or mounting fixtures. If leaks do turn up, drain the branch or system again and resolder the defective joints.

Running the Pipes

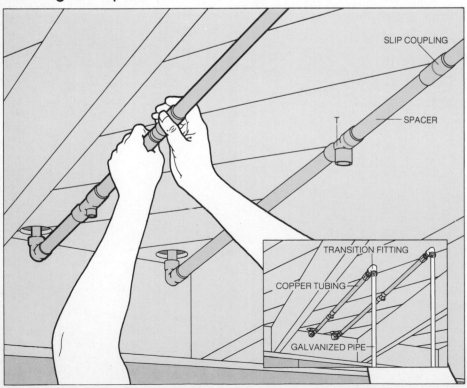

Tapping the supply line. Shut off the water supply and drain the branch you will tap. Cut out an 8-inch section of copper supply pipe. Install a T, angled to receive the first section of the new run, to one of the cut ends and slide a slip coupling over the other. Cut a spacer to fill the remaining opening (you can, if you wish, shorten the section of pipe you cut out). Slip one end of the spacer into the T and set the other against the cut edge of the supply pipe, then slide the slip coupling over the joint, center it and solder it in place. Solder the spacer and the T.

To tap into galvanized steel pipe *(inset)*, remove a section of the pipe between the fittings and replace it with an assembly consisting of two lengths of copper tubing and a T. Attach the tubing to the galvanized pipe with transition fittings *(page 116)*.

SLIP COUPLING

SPACER

T

TRANSITION FITTING

COPPER TUBING

GALVANIZED PIPE

Installing the shutoff valves. Use stop and waste valves as shutoffs for the new supply lines. (Use the valve's waste outlet to drain the new branch for maintenance or repairs.) Solder each valve upright or slanting upward in a section of horizontal pipe closer to the beginning of a run. (A valve with a handle that points downward can easily be clogged with sediment.) To make each installation, open a valve completely, then solder its inlet to the sections of pipe nearest the tapped line and its outlet to the next section of pipe. When the solder cools, close the new valves, restore the water supply to the branch you have tapped and go on with your work on the new supply branch.

Running pipes under a duct. Route the new lines at least 2 inches away from heating and air-conditioning ducts to minimize temperature changes inside the pipes. At one of the bottom corners of the U-shaped pipe trap around the duct, solder a threaded adapter to a T, install the T, and screw a cap on to the adapter. To drain the trap, simply unscrew the cap.

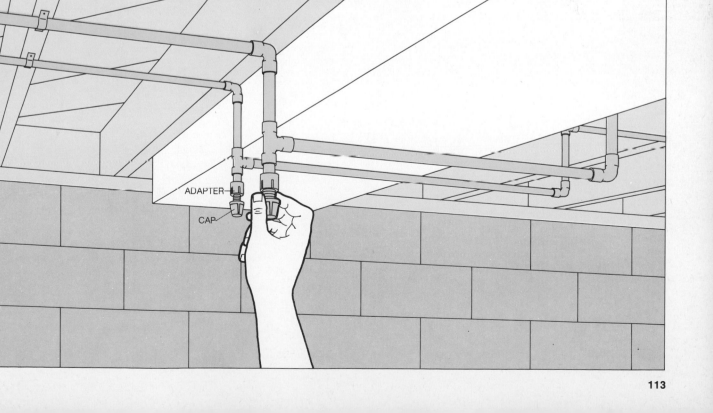

ASBESTOS

STOP AND WASTE VALVE

WASTE OUTLET

ADAPTER

CAP

Lines for Every Fixture

1 The toilet. Run the hot- and cold-water supply lines up through holes in the wet-wall sole plate *(page 97)*; keep the pipes parallel and 6 inches apart, and run the hot-water line to a point 6 inches above the cold. Run a ¾-inch cold-water line horizontally along the rear studs to the toilet location, clamping it to each stud, then bring it through the wall at the rough-in height of the toilet-bowl inlet. To bring the pipe through the wall, attach a ¾-by-½-by-½-inch reducing T to the line at the rough-in point of the toilet inlet. Cut a length of ½-inch tubing to extend 4 inches beyond the finished wall and attach it to the T branch. Seal a test cap to the end.

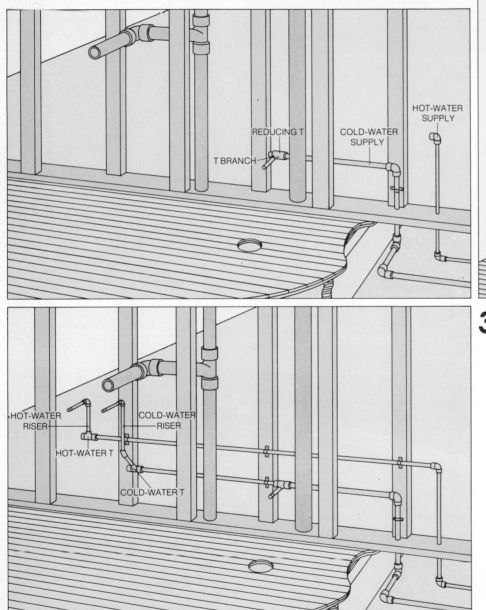

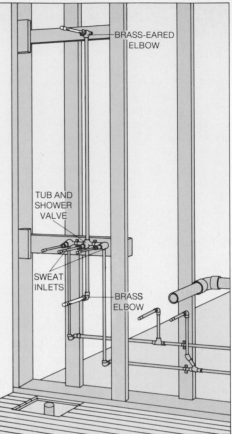

3 The tub and shower. Clamp a tub-and-shower valve body to the framing behind the rough-in points of the tub and shower. Run ½-inch hot- and cold-water supply lines horizontally along the rear studs to points below and behind the valve inlets. Install 90° elbows, pointing out and up at a 45° angle, at the ends of the lines. Run extensions from these elbows to the points below the inlets. Complete the risers with 45° elbows at the ends of the extensions and hot and cold risers to the valve body. Attach the risers to the valve.

Run ½-inch tubing from the shower outlet of the valve to the rough-in point of the shower. Attach a ½-inch brass-eared elbow—a preformed assembly consisting of an elbow and a mounting plate—to the top of the tubing and fasten the elbow to the shower framing. To the threaded outlet of the elbow, screw a capped, threaded test nipple long enough to extend 4 inches beyond the finished wall.

Run ½-inch tubing from the tub-filler outlet of the valve to the rough-in point of the tub filler. Attach a ½-inch elbow to the tubing. To the threaded outlet of the elbow, screw a capped, threaded test nipple long enough to extend 4 inches beyond the finished wall.

Test the entire installation by the method described on page 112.

2 The lavatory. Run a ½-inch cold-water supply line from the toilet T to a point beneath the cold-water rough-in point of the lavatory *(above, left)*, and a ½-inch hot-water supply from its entrance in the wet wall to the hot-water rough-in point. (Because the cold-water line runs close to the floor plate to supply the toilet, run the hot-water line above it.) Start a cold-water riser with a T pointing out and up at a 45° angle, add ½-inch tubing long enough to clear the hot-water line by 6 inches, and connect to it a 45° ½-inch elbow pointing straight up. To start a hot-water riser, attach a ½-inch T to the line. Fit the hot-water T and the cold-water elbow with ½-inch risers that extend 4 inches beyond the finished wall. Seal the ends with test caps.

Increasing the Flow of Water

If water just barely trickles from one faucet, the problem may be nothing more than a clogged aerator. But if trickles are all you get at any fixture in the bathroom or kitchen, the cause may be hard to find. It can be as simple as a main shutoff valve mistakenly left half closed. More often, the problem is due to either of two causes. One is outside the house: inadequate pressure in city mains or a private well system; the other is inside: restricted flow because of clogged, undersized or improperly fitted supply pipes.

There is little you can do to raise the pressure in a water company's main, but you can readily restore or raise the pressure in a private supply system (page 117). On either system, you can clean valves and substitute pipes and fittings less likely to clog (page 116).

If your home is served by a public utility, you can determine the approximate pressure in the city mains by calling the water company. To make sure water is actually reaching your house at that pressure, take a pressure reading (right) in the basement. When taking readings, remember that pressure drops throughout the entire water system during the morning and evening, periods of peak demand. Check whether your neighbors are experiencing a loss of pressure; if not, a significantly lower pressure reading in your home could indicate a leak in the service pipe between the city main and your house. If other evidence, such as a soggy area on the front lawn, seems to confirm this suspicion, ask the water company to investigate—replacing the underground part of the service main, for any reason, is a job generally left to professionals.

On a private well system (page 117), pressure is supplied by a cushion of air that is trapped and compressed at the top of the pressure tank. Should the air leak through a hole in the tank or a faulty fitting, or should it become absorbed by the water, the tank will fill with water and the pump will have to work harder to maintain pressure. Correcting a water-logged tank may be as simple as draining the tank or replacing an air-control valve. And you can raise the pressure in a private system by making a simple adjustment at the pressure switch.

Once you have established that water pressure is adequate, take a flow test (right) at the fixture nearest the service main. If the flow rate turns out to be low, the pipe may be clogged with rust or lime deposits, or it may be undersized (a ½-inch service main, perhaps, instead of the ¾-inch or 1-inch size generally recommended). Galvanized pipes, which generally last about 20 years, are most likely to clog with rust, but if you live in an area with hard water, the interior diameter of any type of piping may be reduced by calcium or lime deposits.

If the pressure and flow tests, taken together, indicate that the problem is inside the house, begin to locate the trouble spot by looking for exterior signs of rust at valves and fittings on the indoor sections of galvanized service mains. Open the pipe at unions to inspect the interior for rust or lime. If you find clogged pipes, replace those that are accessible—generally the horizontal sections in the basement feeding the riser pipes that carry the water to the floors above. Constricted pipes are best replaced with copper tubing; insulating fittings called dielectric unions (page 116) reduce corrosion if copper must be joined to old steel pipes.

Check all valves for mineral deposits. Clean the valve bodies and seats (page 116) and be sure the main shutoff is a gate valve; if a globe valve has been installed on the service main, replacing it with a gate valve will increase the rate of flow at that important point.

Diagnosing the Problem

Measuring water pressure. For a private well system, take a reading on the gauge—normally mounted on the pump (below), tank or connecting piping—just after the pump has shut off. If your system has no gauge, or if the tank is located in a well house, take a reading at a sillcock or laundry faucet with a gauge, sold at plumbing-supply houses, that fits onto a hose adapter (inset). Use this instrument also to check pressure from city mains. Take several readings a day—at both peak and low demand periods—on three successive days, then average all the readings to get the available pressure.

Minimum Flow Rates

Fixture	Gallons per minute
Laundry tub	5
Sillcock	5
Kitchen sink	4.5
Lavatory	3
Bathtub faucet	6
Shower	5
Toilet tank	3

Taking flow tests. These minimum satisfactory flow rates for a variety of fixtures, based on plumbing codes and private surveys, can help you to locate badly clogged branch pipes or warn you that the entire plumbing system is constricted. Beginning at the basement fixtures closest to the service main and working your way upstairs, remove aerators or other flow-restricting devices and use a stop watch to measure the time taken to fill a 10-gallon pail. Divide the time in minutes into 10 to calculate the flow in gallons per minute. If only one or two fixtures give readings close to or lower than the chart minimums, check these branch pipes for undersizing or clogging. If all the readings are low, replacing the horizontal pipe runs in the basement (page 116) may help.

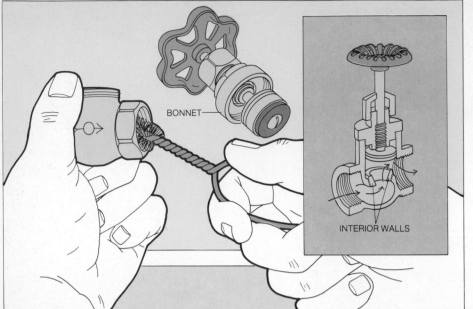

Clearing the Passages through Valves and Pipes

Cleaning a globe valve. A stiff wire brush—called a copper-fitting cleaning brush—is the best tool to use to loosen and remove mineral particles lodged against the interior walls of a valve. To get the valve apart, first close the nearest valve on the inlet side and drain water from the first tap beyond the discharge side. Then open the pipe at a nearby union and unscrew the valve. If the valve is close to a joist or wall, you may have to unscrew the bonnet in order to rotate the valve body; otherwise, separate the bonnet from the body at a workbench. When you reinstall the valve make sure the arrow on the body points in the direction of water flow *(inset)*.

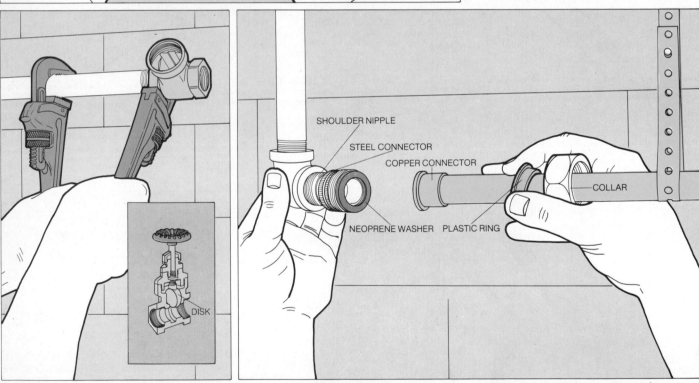

Installing a gate valve. If the main shutoff on your service pipe is a globe valve, replace it with a gate valve, using one wrench to hold the pipe and a second wrench to work the valve. A globe valve slows water by channeling it through an S-shaped path, while a gate valve's base houses a vertical disk that rises to allow a direct passage *(inset)* with less pressure loss. Before starting work, shut off the water at the street or at the pressure tank, drain the system and open the nearest union on the house side of the valve. To avoid leakage and mineral build-up, install the valve with the handle upward or sideways.

Replacing clogged pipes. To substitute new copper tubing for clogged galvanized pipe, remove accessible horizontal runs, disconnecting them at the elbows or Ts that connect to risers. Replace the rusted Ts and elbows with new galvanized fittings. Then, using shoulder nipples, connect the steel to the copper with special transition fittings called dielectric unions, which reduce the corrosion.

The unions consist of five separate pieces: a threaded steel connector for the galvanized pipe; a copper connector that must be soldered to

the tubing; a steel union collar to tighten both connectors; and a neoprene washer and a plastic insulating ring that separate the two metals to prevent corrosion. To avoid damaging the fitting as you solder the copper connector, turn the steel connector and neoprene washer aside *(above)*, and slide the plastic ring and union collar down the copper tube. After soldering, realign the steel connector, slide the plastic ring flush with the flange on the copper connector and tighten the collar. Then secure the tubing to the joists, replacing the old straps with copper-clad pipe hooks or hanger straps.

Boosting the Pressure of a Private Well

Resetting the pressure switch. Inadequate flow from a well may be due to a low pressure setting. If the pressure switch, tank and pump are rated for a pressure higher than the setting of the switch, try raising the high, or cutout, setting of the switch by 5 pounds. Maximum ratings are usually printed on plates of all components; if they are not, get the figures from the distributor.

Before removing the cover, turn off the power. In the typical switch illustrated, a large range spring adjusts both cutin and cutout pressures simultaneously, and a smaller differential spring changes the cutout setting. To raise the cutout pressure 5 pounds, move the differential spring adjusting nut clockwise, as viewed from above the switch, slightly less than two full turns. Replace the cover, restore power and observe the pump through one operating cycle to see that adjusted pressure reaches, but does not exceed, the desired level.

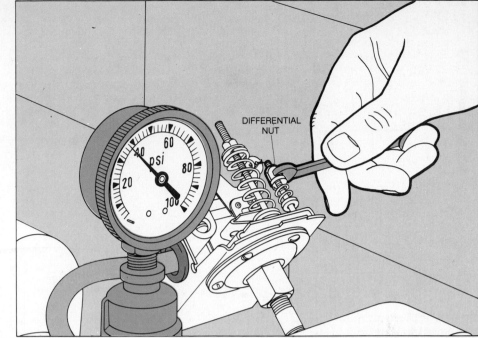

DIFFERENTIAL NUT

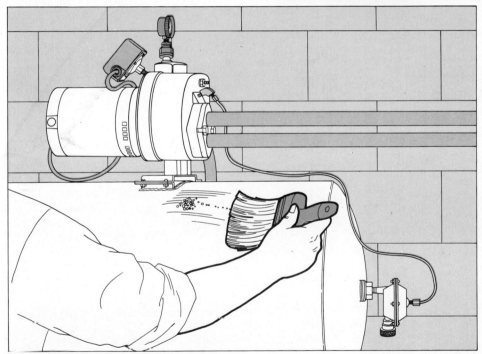

Finding air leaks in pressure tanks. Fluctuating water flow suggests a waterlogged or leaking tank. To check it for leaks, coat its upper half and fittings with a soapy solution; if you see bubbles, tighten fittings or, if the tank walls leak, replace the tank. But waterlogging is a more likely cause of fluctuations—an older tank can become waterlogged every 6 months as air is absorbed by water. To recharge, shut off the pump and drain the tank by opening the drain cock and a house faucet so that air will enter.

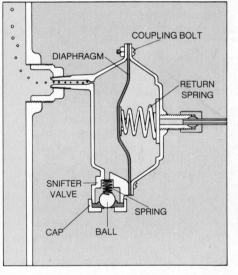

COUPLING BOLT

DIAPHRAGM

RETURN SPRING

SNIFTER VALVE

SPRING

CAP   BALL

Repairing an air-volume control. One cause of frequent waterlogging is a defective air-volume control. The model shown here sucks air through a snifter valve when the pump starts, then forces the air into the tank with a spring-loaded rubber diaphragm when the pump stops. Worn parts in a control can be replaced from repair kits, which are supplied by manufacturers and wholesalers.

To disassemble the control, turn off electric power to the pump, drain the tank and loosen the control's coupling bolts. Separate the halves, taking care not to kink the flexible copper tubing between control and pump (this tubing is visible in the drawing at left). Unscrew the remaining control half from the tank and loosen the knurled cap holding the snifter valve assembly. Replace the valve seat, ball and spring.

The Final Step: Connecting the Fixtures

Once the framing and rough-in plumbing are in place, installing kitchen and bathroom fixtures is mostly a matter of positioning and connecting supply pipes and drainpipes. With most bathtubs, toilets and sinks, installing new fixtures simply reverses the procedures used to remove the old ones *(pages 90-93)*. You will need the same tools plus a tube cutter or hacksaw to cut pipe.

Most pipe connections require little more than the tightening of slip nuts. But take care not to damage any of the parts by overtightening nuts—always hand-tighten them first, then make an extra quarter turn with a wrench.

Use plumber's putty where you want watertight seals and apply pipe-joint compound or joint tape to threaded connections, plastic as well as metal. Check

your work by turning on the water and searching for leaks with your fingers as well as your eyes.

While most fixtures are installed after floors and walls are finished, bathtubs should go in before, since tubs usually rest on the subfloor and are secured to the wall by vertical flange supports nailed to the studs. If you are using a steel or fiberglass tub, which makes more noise than a cast-iron tub when struck by water, you can reduce the racket by laying fiberglass insulation on the subfloor.

Setting a tub snugly into a three-wall enclosure requires some careful movements by at least two people—four if a heavy cast-iron tub is to be installed. It takes less effort to place a tub with a finished end against two walls; the job is easier yet if only the tub's long side ad-

joins a wall, but you may have to build a rim-high wood cover at the head end to protect—and conceal—the supply pipes and drainpipes, which are usually connected as soon as the tub is firmly positioned. The faucet spout, handles and shower arm, not connected to the tub, are added after the walls around the tub are finished. Somewhat different techniques are used when a prefabricated tub enclosure is installed *(pages 124-125)*.

Compared to a bathtub installation, putting in a new toilet *(pages 120-121)* is a simple, one-man job. Most parts are supplied by the manufacturer but you must provide a flange sized to your waste pipe; a wax gasket to seal the connection between bowl and flange; a set of closet bolts, nuts and washers; and a flexible supply pipe to connect the shutoff valve.

Installing a Bathtub

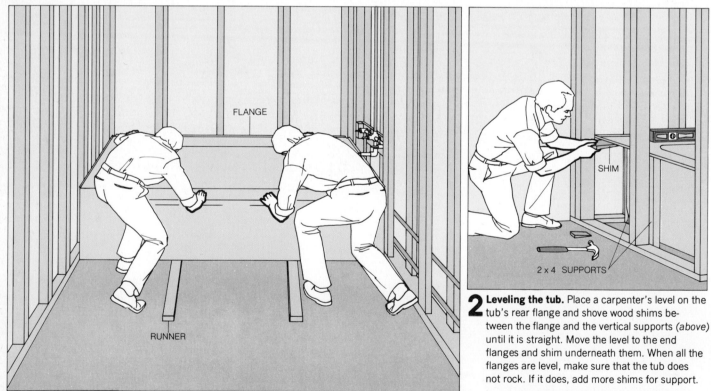

1 Positioning the tub. To lift and shove a lightweight fiberglass or steel bathtub into a framed enclosure, you will need at least one helper. For a heavier cast-iron tub, lay a pair of 2-by-4 runners on the subfloor leading into the framed enclosure and enlist three helpers to set the tub on the 2-by-4s. Two men

can then push the tub into the enclosure *(above)*. Ease out the 2-by-4s, letting the bathtub settle onto the subfloor and its flanges onto the vertical supports. The waterproof wallboard will rest on the flange of the tub and the tile or other finish wall covering will rest on the rim of the bathtub.

2 Leveling the tub. Place a carpenter's level on the tub's rear flange and shove wood shims between the flange and the vertical supports *(above)* until it is straight. Move the level to the end flanges and shim underneath them. When all the flanges are level, make sure that the tub does not rock. If it does, add more shims for support.

Nail or screw the flanges of steel or fiberglass tubs to the studs. If there are no holes, drive large-headed roofing nails into the studs just above the flanges, so that their heads pin the flange and hold it securely. Cast-iron tubs need not be nailed to the stud wall; their weight keeps them in place.

3 **Attaching the drainpipes.** Unscrew and remove the chrome overflow plate, the lift linkage, the strainer cap and the crosspiece. Connect the waste and overflow pipes with a slip nut and washer, and set them on the waste T. Place the large beveled washer between the back of the tub and the overflow pipe. Place the large flat washer between the drainpipe and the bottom of the tub. Position the assembly and tighten the slip nuts that lock it into place. Roll some plumber's putty into a strand about 7 inches long and ¼ inch thick. Press the putty around the underside of the crosspiece before screwing it by hand into the tub's drain hole *(below)* and tightening it with pliers handles and pry bar *(page 92)*. Then screw down the strainer cap. Protect the tub surface with dropcloths or paper while you finish the tub walls.

4 **Adjusting the lift linkage.** Loosen the lock nut *(below)* to turn the threaded rod that shortens or lengthens the linkage used to open and close the drain. Adjust the linkage to the position specified by the manufacturer and tighten the lock nut. Slip the linkage into the overflow hole and reattach the overflow plate.

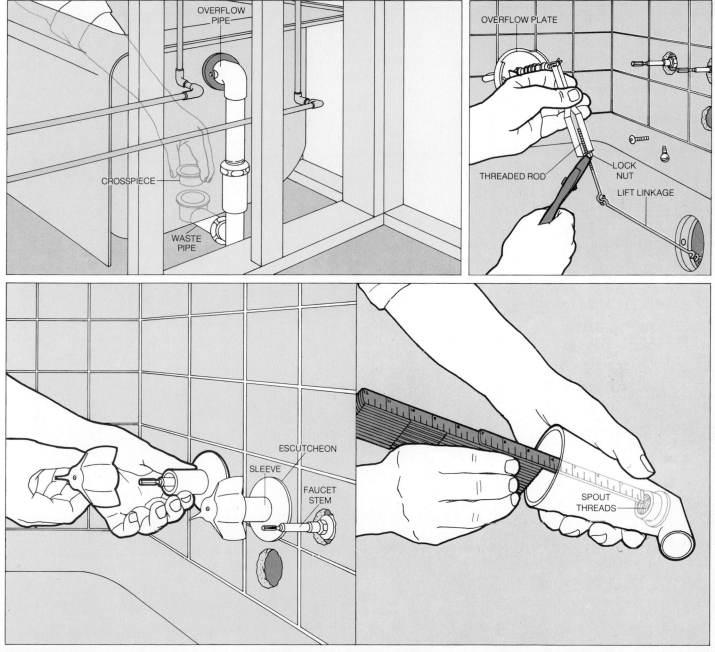

5 **Connecting hardware.** To install most faucet or diverter-valve handles, slide escutcheons and sleeves onto the protruding stems *(above)* before screwing on the handles. For other types of handles, including single-lever controls, follow the manufacturer's instructions. Before mounting the spout, measure from the face of the elbow behind the wall to the face of the wall; add the distance from the threads in the spout to the end of the spout, plus ¾ inch *(above, right)*. Remove the rough-in nipple and replace it with a nipple of the measurement you have made. Use only brass or galvanized steel for the new nipple. Apply a coat of joint compound to the threads of the nipple and screw on the spout as tightly as possible with your hands.

To install a shower arm, remove the nipple from the supply pipe. Apply joint compound to the threads of the arm, place the escutcheon over the arm and screw the arm to the pipe by hand.

Hooking Up a Toilet

1 **Attaching a shutoff valve.** If no shutoff valve exists at the desired location, cut the supply pipe 2 inches from the wall. Slide an escutcheon over the pipe and press it against the wall opening. Slip the coupling nut and compression ring over the pipe. Slide on the valve *(right)*, its outlet hole pointing up, and tighten the nut.

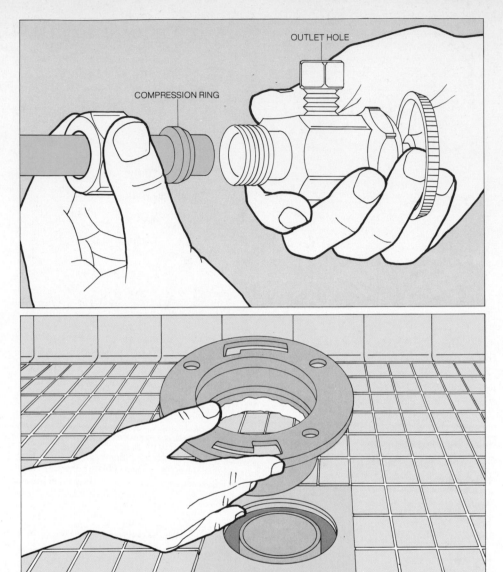

2 **Seating the flange.** Use a plastic flange with a plastic waste pipe. Cement inside the flange stem and outside the waste pipe, then push the flange onto the pipe. Drill holes into the subfloor through the screw holes and secure the flange to the floor with flathead wood screws.

3 **Attaching the wax gasket.** Turn the toilet bowl upside down on padding. Slip the doughnut-shaped wax gasket over the ridge around the waste hole. Press it firmly against the bowl bottom and ridge with your fingers *(right)*.

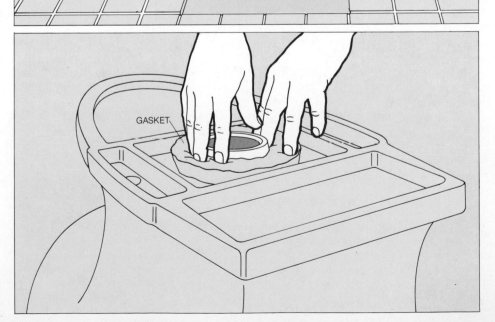

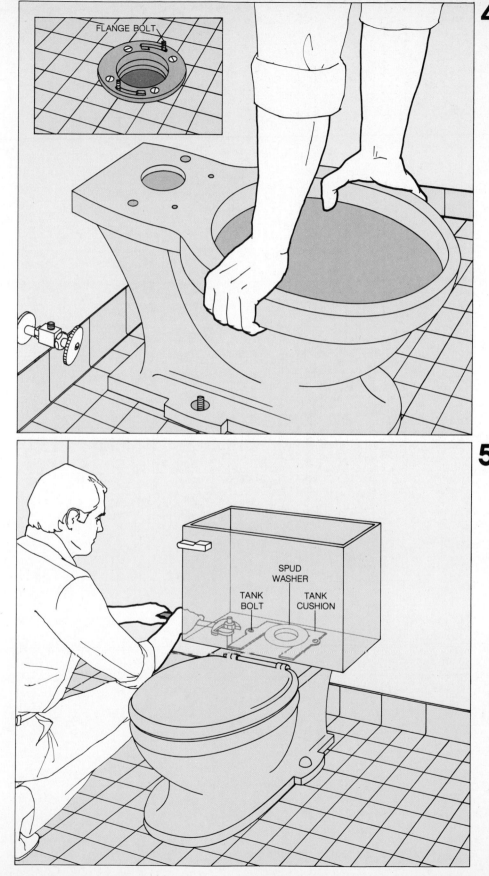

FLANGE BOLT

4 **Setting the bowl.** Insert and position the two flange bolts (*inset*). Lift the bowl and lower it slowly onto the flange so that the bolts protrude through the bowl's rim holes. Press down firmly on the bowl (*left*) while twisting it slightly in both directions to seal the gasket. Place a level across the width and then the depth of the upper rim. Shim if necessary with copper or brass washers beneath the lower rim, but do not raise the bowl or the gasket seal will be broken. Place washers on the flange bolts before tightening the nuts just enough to keep the bowl from moving. Place porcelain caps over the bolt ends.

5 **Connecting the tank and supply line.** If the tank is a separate unit, make certain that the spud washer and tank cushion are in place before sealing the tank so that the two tank bolts pass through holes in the bowl's rim. Attach the tank with washers and nuts from below. Then attach the seat and cover assembly.

Select the correct diameter flexible supply pipe recommended by the toilet manufacturer. Hold the head of the supply pipe against the tank's threaded inlet stem while bending the pipe slowly to form a gentle curve past the shutoff valve. Mark the pipe where it passes the bottom threads of the shutoff valve and cut the pipe with a tube cutter. Slip a coupling nut up the pipe and hand-fasten it to the inlet stem. Slip on the valve coupling nut and compression ring before inserting the pipe into the valve and tightening both nuts (*left*). Turn on the valve, flush the toilet and check for leaks.

SPUD WASHER

TANK BOLT

TANK CUSHION

Three Fixtures for a Kitchen

The kitchen's three basic plumbing fixtures—sink, garbage disposal and dishwasher—are almost a single unit for installation purposes, since the disposal is an extension of the sink drain and all three share a single waste pipe. With proper preparation, the three installations are mostly a matter of tightening nuts and screws.

The easiest way to mount a sink is to attach as many fittings—faucets, strainer, spray hose, tailpiece—as possible before setting the sink into the countertop. This minimizes the difficulty of working in a cramped space.

A disposal requires wiring to a convenient wall switch. Once the wiring is installed and tested, it takes only a few minutes to fasten the disposal to the sink, and to connect the wires *(Step 4)*.

Dishwashers *(opposite)* have three connections: a hot-water supply line, tapped from the sink line and equipped with its own shut-off valve; a waste line tapped to the drain or disposal; and an electrical connection to a 120-volt circuit *(page 55)*. All three connections are made through an access panel at the lower front after the dishwasher is positioned. Many local codes require air gaps for dishwasher waste lines to prevent siphonage of waste water back into the cleaning chamber. If you need an air gap, be sure your sink has a precut hole. Otherwise you may have to drill a hole through a steel sink or a countertop.

Combining a Sink and Disposal

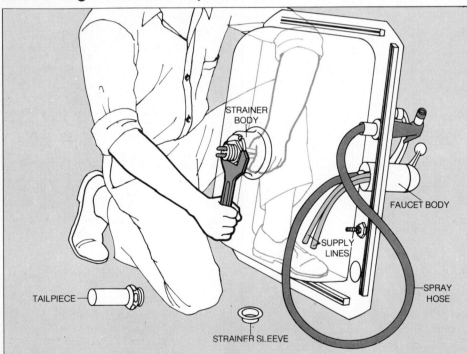

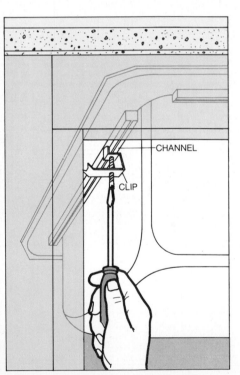

1 Attaching the fittings. Prop the sink on its side for ready access to top and bottom. If the faucet body comes with a rubber gasket, slip it over the stems; otherwise apply a ⅛-inch bead of plumber's putty around the body base before sliding the stems through the holes provided. You may have to partly straighten attached copper supply lines by bending them slowly. If a spray hose is provided, follow the manufacturer's instructions when attaching it to the faucet body and the designated sink opening. For a sink without a garbage disposal (a disposal installation is shown in Step 4, opposite), apply a ⅛-inch bead of plumber's putty to the underside of the strainer body lip before setting it into the drain hole. Slip the rubber and metal washers and a lock nut onto the threaded bottom of the strainer body. Hand-tighten the lock nut. Insert the handles of a pair of pliers into the hole from the top surface to keep the strainer body from turning before tightening (above). Then assemble the strainer sleeve, lock nut and tailpiece and attach the tailpiece to the strainer body.

2 Attaching the sink. Apply a ¼-inch bead of plumber's putty around the top edge of the countertop opening. Lower the sink into the opening. From underneath, slide at least eight evenly spaced clips into channels that rim the sink underside and position them to grip the underside of the countertop. Tighten the clips with a screwdriver (above) but do not overtighten or you may crimp the sink rim. Afterward, check the top for a good seal between the sink rim and the countertop; if there are any high spots, adjust the clips to pull them down.

3 **Connecting the pipes.** Attach shutoff valves to the stub-outs *(page 120)*. If the faucet body has supply pipes attached, fasten them to the valves in the same way you would a toilet supply *(page 121)*. If the pipes are not long enough—or if there are none—use compression couplings to attach copper tubing *(below)*.

Uncap the drainpipe and add a coupling. If the drainpipe is chrome, use a plastic-chrome adapter. For a disposal, follow the instructions in Step 4 below; otherwise, slide a slip nut and washer onto the tailpiece. Adjust the drainpipe so that the trap fits properly, making a trial assembly, then cement the drain to the coupling. Slide an escutcheon, slip nut and washer over the drainpipe and install the trap.

Running Lines for a Dishwasher

1 **Connecting the dishwasher.** Prepare the dishwasher space by running in electrical cable from an adjoining wall, and by drilling or cutting a 6-inch hole in the lower rear of any cabinet wall separating the dishwasher space from the sink space. Run a length of flexible copper tubing and the dishwasher drain hose through the hole, along with the electrical cable if necessary. Remove the access panel and kick plate from the lower front of the dishwasher before pushing the dishwasher into its opening. If the leveling legs are not accessible through the access panel, you may have to pull out and push back the dishwasher several

times to level the unit flush with the countertop. The connections can then be made with the dishwasher in or out of its space.

Use a compression fitting to connect the copper tubing to the inlet pipe. Use a hose clamp to connect the drain hose to the outlet pipe. Push the dishwasher into its space and screw it to the countertop through precut holes in front. Connect the wiring and replace the access panel and kick plate. Attach the other end of the tubing to the sink hot-water pipe with a separate shutoff valve, and the drain hose to the sink tailpiece or air gap *(bottom, center)*.

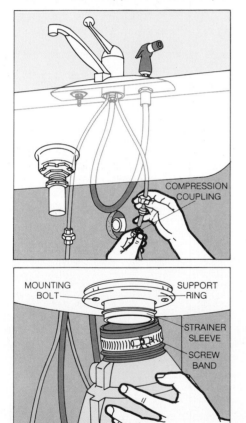

COMPRESSION COUPLING

MOUNTING BOLT · SUPPORT RING · STRAINER SLEEVE · SCREW BAND

4 **Attaching a disposal.** With the sink dismounted, insert the disposal strainer in place of the strainer body *(Step 1)*. Slide on the rubber and metal gaskets and loosely thread the mounting bolts before snapping on the support ring. Tighten the bolts, but do not buckle the support ring. After the sink is mounted *(Step 2)*, place the clamp around the disposal collar and lift the disposal *(above)* so it locks into the strainer sleeve. Install a small P trap to join the disposal waste pipe to the drain. Tighten the clamp before connecting the electricity.

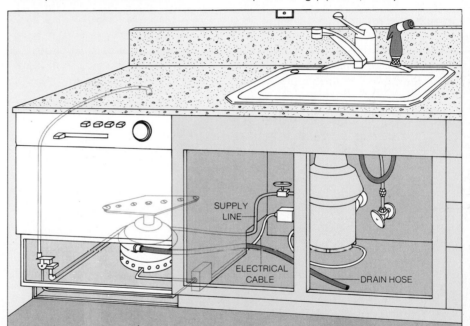

SUPPLY LINE

ELECTRICAL CABLE · DRAIN HOSE

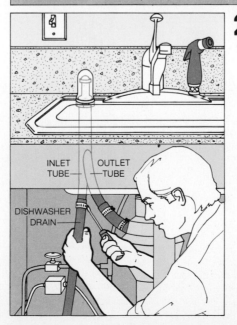

INLET TUBE · OUTLET TUBE

DISHWASHER DRAIN

2 **Connecting the air gap.** If an air gap is required, raise the stem from below through a hole in the sink or countertop, screw on the plastic top and press in the chrome outer cap. Fasten the dishwasher drain hose to the inlet tube of the air gap with a hose clamp *(left)*. Connect the outlet tube to the disposal, using a section of hose and clamps, or to the tailpiece of the sink, using a Y connector. On some disposals, you may have to punch in a knockout plug at the top, then retrieve the plug with a pair of long-nose pliers.

A Prefab Tub-and-Wall Unit

Prefabricated fiberglass tub enclosures, lightweight and easy to install, usually consist of a tub and three surrounding walls in a one-piece unit or in four-piece packages. Because the one-piece units are too large to fit through a standard doorway they usually must be positioned before the bathroom is framed in. Four-piece enclosures, more practical in existing bathrooms, can be brought inside unassembled and then snapped or clipped together at the installation site. Prefabricated shower stalls, which are similarly installed, require the preparation of a special floor drain.

Because the parts of a prefabricated enclosure must fit precisely, the framework should be perfectly square and plumb. Some manufacturers require additional horizontal or vertical framing for greater rigidity. If the enclosure is not already backed with factory-sprayed insulation to deaden splashing noise, regular household insulation can be stapled to the framing and laid on the subfloor.

Fiberglass can be cut and drilled with woodworking tools, but it cracks easily under stress and should be handled with care. Always drill starter holes before nailing into the material.

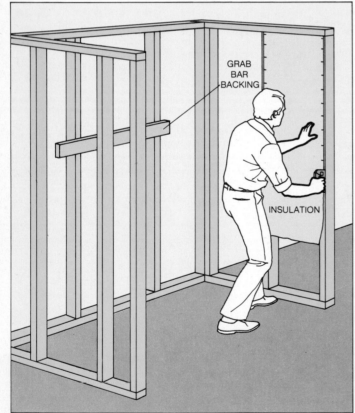

1 **Framing the enclosure.** Follow the manufacturer's framing specifications, which may call for additional supports like the horizontal backing for a grab bar. With one-piece units, which must be slid into the framework, you may get maneuvering room by not nailing the two outer studs on the foot end until after installation—provided that you have access from the other side. Staple soundproofing insulation to the studs (*above*) and lay additional insulation on the subfloor, in thicknesses specified by the manufacturer.

2 **Measuring for openings.** If possible, mark the locations of faucet stems, diverter valve stem, spout nipple and shower elbow directly on the appropriate panel by dry-fitting it against the rough-in plumbing. Where this is impractical, as in the case of a fully assembled enclosure, use a stud to mark the distance from floor to each opening on a single vertical line. Measure the horizontal distances from this line and transfer the markings to the face of the enclosure (*above*). Drill holes with a spade bit from the face side.

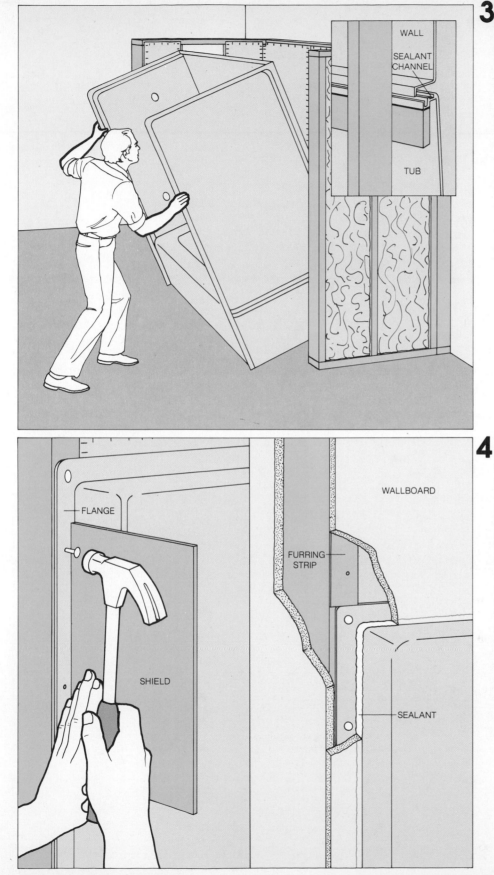

3 **Positioning the enclosure.** If the enclosure is a one-piece or fully assembled unit, slide it through the wall from the foot end, if possible, and position the openings at the opposite end before nailing the missing studs. Otherwise the enclosure must be positioned from the face of the framework *(left)*, making it necessary to temporarily unscrew protruding plumbing. Tilt the unit so the bottom of the front flange rests across the opening of the framework, then lower the other end and work it flush against the rear studs.

If the enclosure comes in four pieces, position the tub first. Then lay a bead of sealant in the sealant channels, if there are any, and attach the walls to the tub and to one another *(inset)*. Some installations may require clips to be attached from the rear. Use shims to plumb and level the enclosure before connecting the plumbing *(page 119)*.

WALL

SEALANT CHANNEL

TUB

4 **Nailing and finishing.** Fiberglass cracks easily, so predrill holes if necessary before securing the enclosure to the studs with roofing nails. Use a shield of cardboard or thin plywood when hammering to protect adjacent fiberglass surfaces *(opposite)*. To close off the space—about 2 feet—above the enclosure, nail ⅛-inch furring strips to the exposed portions of studs. Apply a ⅜-inch bead of sealant—equal to the thickness of wallboard—inside the top flange, as shown in the cutaway at left. Measure and cut a piece of wallboard and set the lower edge into the sealant. Then nail the wallboard to the studs through the furring strips. Cover the vertical flanges on either side by lapping them with wallboard panels or, when adjacent walls join the enclosure at right angles, as shown here, by cementing a thin strip of wallboard. Finally, apply sealant to the openings and attach the plumbing hardware.

FLANGE

SHIELD

WALLBOARD

FURRING STRIP

SEALANT

Picture Credits

The sources for the illustrations in this book are shown below. Credits for the pictures from left to right are separated by semicolons, from top to bottom by dashes.

Cover—Fred Maroon. 6—Fred Maroon. 8, 9—Drawings by Peter McGinn. 10 through 13—Drawings by Fred Bigio from B-C Graphics. 14 through 19—Drawings by Gerry Gallagher. 20, 21—Laszlo L. Bodrogi from Artograph Associates. 23 through 27—Drawings by Peter McGinn. 28, 29—Drawings by Dick Gage. 30 through 35—Drawings by Fred Bigio from B-C Graphics. 36 through 39—Drawings by Peter McGinn. 40—Fred Maroon. 42 through 45—Drawings by Adolph E. Brotman. 46 through 49—Drawings by Ray Skibinski. 50, 51—Drawings by Fred Bigio from B-C Graphics. 53 through 55—Drawings by Whitman Studio, Inc. 56 through 59—Drawings by Gerry Gallagher. 60 through 63—Drawings by Vicki Vebell. 64 through 68—Drawings by Gerry Gallagher. 69 through 71—Drawings by Peter McGinn. 72, 73—Drawings by Vicki Vebell. 74—Fred Maroon. 79—Drawing by Vantage Art, Inc. 81 through 83—Drawings by Whitman Studio, Inc. 84 through 87—Drawings by Vantage Art, Inc. 88A—Maris/Semel, Julian and Barbara Neski, Architects. Home of Mr. and Mrs. Stephen Kaplan. 88B, 88C—Carla De Benedetti, Gae Aulenti, Architects—Rob Super, Peters, Clayberg & Caulfield, Architects; Graham Henderson from Elizabeth Whiting, Nicholas Hills, Architect. 88D—Norman McGrath, courtesy of "Interior Design Magazines," Charles Mount, Designer—Tim Street Porter from Elizabeth Whiting, Barney Broadbent, Designer. 88E—Maris/Semel, Michael Lax, Designer. 88F—Roger Gain from Mitchell Beazley; Michael Boys from Susan Griggs Agency—Ed Stoecklein, Stern & Hagman, Architects; Robert Perron, Robert Shaw, Designer. 88G—Maris/Semel, courtesy of "House Beautiful," ©1975, The Hearst Corporation, Alan Buchsbaum, Architect. 88H—Fil Hunter. 90 through 93—Drawings by Adolph E. Brotman. 94 through 99—Drawings by Nicholas Fasciano. 100 through 103—Drawings by Great, Inc. 104 through 107—Drawings by Peter McGinn. 108 through 114—Drawings by John Massey. 115 through 117—Drawings by Fred Bigio from B-C Graphics. 118 through 125—Drawings by Vicki Vebell.

The following persons also assisted in the making of this book: Howard Fields, William Garvey, Don Robertson and William Schremp helped with the writing and research. Roger C. Essley, Fred Collins, Fred Holtz, Joan McGurren, W. F. McWilliam, Lee Nolan and Carol Summar prepared the sketches from which the final illustrations were drawn.

Acknowledgments

The index/glossary for this book was prepared by Mel Ingber. The editors also thank the following: William Berger, Division of Environmental Health, Fairfax County Health Department, Fairfax, Va.; Benny Bianco, Chief Plumbing Inspector, Arlington, Va.; Claude Brewer, Brewer Well Drilling, Galax, Va.; Steve Bulmer, Village Carpets & Interiors, Camp Springs, Md.; James Coughlin, Square D Co., Asheville, N.C.; Raymond L. Crawford, Reed Electric Co., Washington, D.C.; Scott Dyke, Raygold Cabinets, Berryville, Va.; Odette Eaves, Thos. Somerville Co., Washington, D.C.; James G. Euwer II, Armstrong Cork Co., Lancaster, Pa.; Don Fields, Washington, D.C.; Lou Figliosi, Ceramic Tile, Inc., Rockville, Md.; Lelland L. Gallup, Cornell University, Ithaca, N.Y.; Robert Gibbs, CKD, Cox Kitchens & Baths, Baltimore, Md.; Barbara Kuehn, Home Ventilating Institute, Chicago; Walter M. Hite, J. & H. Aitcheson Co., Alexandria, Va.; Alfred L. Hobgood III, The Kitchen Shoppe, Alexandria, Va.; Jack Hutchinson, Hutchinson Glass and Mirror, Inc., Washington, D.C.; Len Koppana, Formco, Inc., Cincinnati; Arnold Craig Levin, Griswold Heckel & Kelly Assoc., Inc., New York City; John Lopynski, Columbia Mirror and Glass of Georgetown, Inc., Washington, D.C.; David Lyon, Macklanburg Duncan Co., Oklahoma City, Okla.; Charles Miller, Mamaroneck, N.Y.; Larry Miller, Tait, Inc., Dayton, Ohio; National Waterwell Assoc., Worthington, Ohio; John O'Boyle, Virginia American Water Co., Alexandria, Va.; Richard Poole, CBI Fairmac Corp., Arlington, Va.; John Purcell, Top Notch Laminates, Rockville, Md.; Louis E. Schucker III, CKD, The Kitchen Guild, Washington, D.C.; Margareta Smith, Viking Sauna Co., San Jose, Calif.; Paul Tatelbaum, Hechinger Co., Washington, D.C.; John P. Weintraub, Frager's Hardware, Washington, D.C.; George Williams, County Department of Environmental Management, Fairfax, Va.; David Wolbrink, Broan Manufacturing Co., Hartford, Wisc.; Joel Yates, Kensington, Md.

Index/Glossary